D1068504

Mr. Daniels and the Grange

by
ERIC SLOANE and
EDWARD ANTHONY

OTHER BOOKS BY ERIC SLOANE

A *Reverence for Wood*

A Sound of Bells

A Museum of Early American Tools

ABC Book of Early Americana

American Barns and Covered Bridges

American Yesterday

Book of Storms

Diary of an Early American Boy: Noah Blake—1805

Eric Sloane's Almanac

Eric Sloane's Weather Book

Folklore of American Weather

Look at the Sky

Our Vanishing Landscape

Return to Taos: A Sketchbook of Roadside Americana

The Seasons of America Past

An Age of Barns

The Cracker Barrel

OTHER BOOKS BY EDWARD ANTHONY

O Rare Don Marquis

This Is Where I Came In

Bring 'Em Back Alive (with Frank Buck)

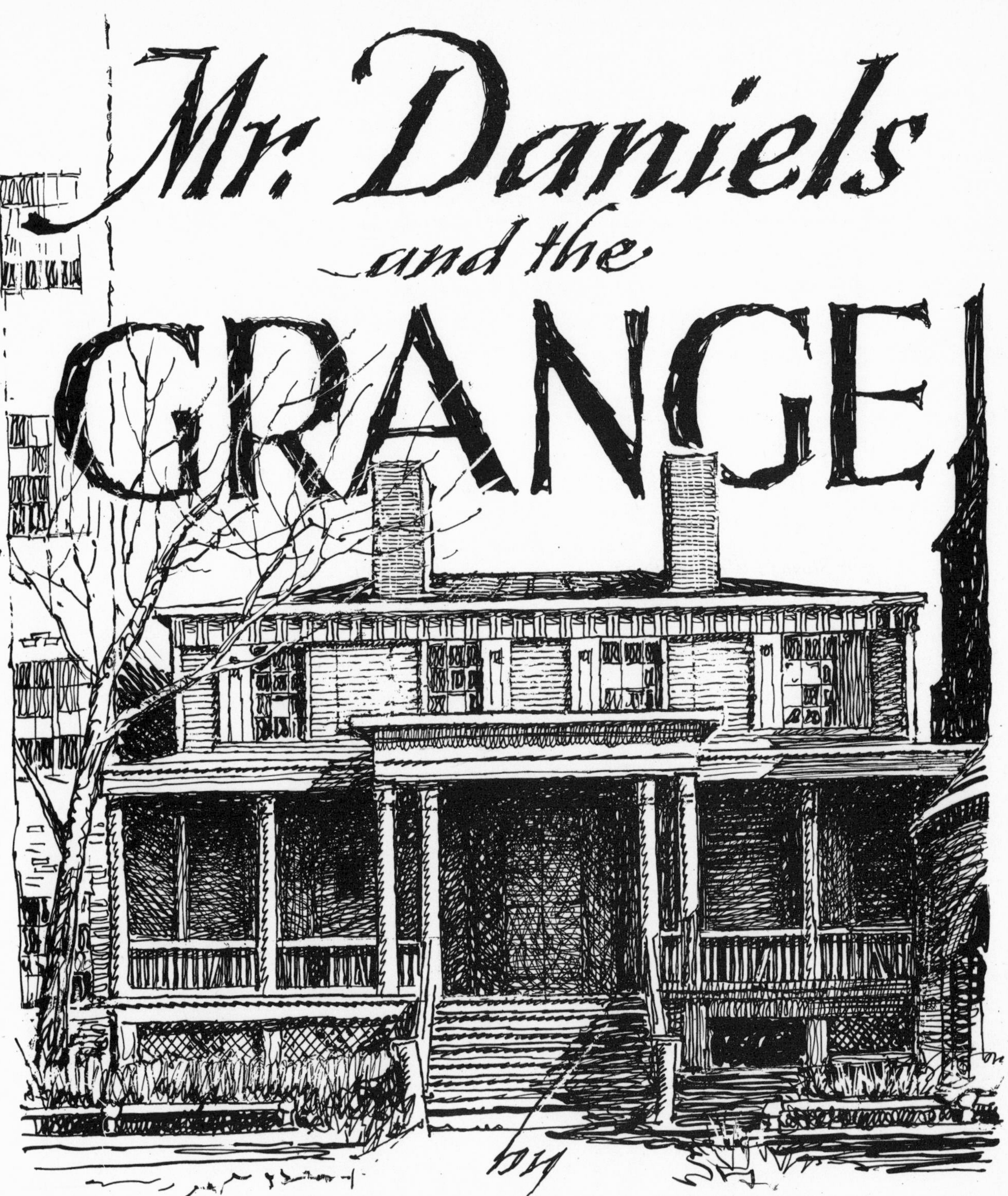

ERIC SLOANE

and

EDWARD ANTHONY

Funk & Wagnalls New York

Library of Congress Catalog Card Number: 68-12006
Published by Funk & Wagnalls, *A Division of* Reader's Digest Books, Inc.

Printed in the United States of America

Foreword

On a bleak November day in 1798 Alexander Hamilton wrote to his wife from a hotel in Philadelphia, "I have formed a sweet project . . . in which I rely that you will cooperate with me cheerfully."

The Hamiltons had never owned a home of their own. Mr. Hamilton's "sweet project" was to build a comfortable house for his family on a hill in what was then the open farm country of upper Manhattan Island. The house, which he called The Grange, was built and occupied by the Hamiltons, but the head of the household had little time to enjoy it. Within a few years he was dead at the hand of Aaron Burr in American history's most tragic duel.

Despite many misfortunes that followed, The Grange has survived. On April 20, 1962, President Kennedy signed the Act of Congress that made it a national memorial and a unit of the National Park System. It will be preserved "to commemorate the historic role played by Alexander Hamilton in the establishment of this Nation."

The Act stipulates that Hamilton's Grange must be moved from its present site; that the new location be lands donated for that purpose; and that the new site be large enough to assure proper interpretation of the building to the visiting public.

Selection of a suitable site has delayed the badly needed work of restoration. The Grange now stands on part of the original Hamilton estate. Its neighbors believe, and the Department of the Interior concurs, that it should remain in this general vicinity. There is reason to hope that this can be worked out. Meanwhile, National Park Service historians and architects have completed exhaustive research that will enable the place to be restored to its original appearance. But little actual restoration has been possible because the structure will have to be cut in half and moved in sections when the time comes for it to be taken to another site.

The story of The Grange is unusually poignant in several ways, from the personal tragedies of the Hamilton family there to the manner in which we Americans allowed this fine historic home to deteriorate. There is poignancy too in the loving care that has been given the place by Raleigh Henry Daniels in more recent years. These vignettes, and others woven into the story, tell us things about our country that enrich our understanding of past and present and help us and our children to understand the future better. This is more than the story of Alexander Hamilton's house alone.

STEWART L. UDALL
Secretary of the Interior

Contents

Mr. Daniels . . . .

by Eric Sloane . .

Mr. Daniels . . .

Hamilton Terrace, when I lived there during the First World War, sat quietly and comfortably between the little shops of higher Amsterdam Avenue and the sprawling gray conglomerate valley of Harlem. It was a three-block-long shelf of stone stairs that pushed each household up and away from the street, respectably above the sidewalks. I remember lace parlor curtains but as I think back I cannot recall ever having seen anyone looking from a front window. It was a street of reserve and calmness broken only occasionally by the delivery of coal rattling down iron chutes that stretched from the trucks across the sidewalks and into the cellars beneath the stoops. The Dutch of Manhattan's Harlem were the first to call a step a "stoop," a name that still persists in New York.

We played stoop ball against the high brownstone steps, but I don't remember any games that involved yelling or loud noises. Sometimes a newsboy came through shouting "Extra! Read all about it!" and he somehow gave the impression of being lost and shouting just from force of habit. About once a year, usually in the spring, boys of the Eighth Avenue gang announced themselves with shrill cries of "Weee-hawkeee!" and as they passed through the street, menacingly carrying sticks and bottles, we watched them from behind the safety of downstairs iron-grilled areaway doors.

There were few other sounds that persist in my memory of those days, but I do remember how on a still day from the rooftops you could hear the hum of the surrounding city and the faraway clatter to the east of the "El" trains in Harlem. I frequently found my way to the roof: somehow I liked to imagine that it was my own private discovery. At least I never encountered anyone else there. The roof could be reached through a hall closet in the upper or "help's floor." In the closet there was a rough wooden ladderlike stairway, and at the top one could push up a boxed lid just far enough to climb through. Then suddenly there was a world of sky and wind faintly odored with coal-gas and the pleasing smell of tarred roofs.

Sometimes I flew kites from the roof, but my specialty was releasing parachutes made of tissue paper. Using flour and water for paste, I glued narrow triangular strips into umbrella shapes, and if I put the minimum of weight at the end of the threads below, instead of falling, the parachute would often be lifted by warm air currents and sail off to the east to land somewhere on the Harlem rooftops. However, it was also fun just to lie on the rooftop and peek over the edge to spy on whatever went on down in the street below. From above, people were just hats with feet that popped in and out in front, but if you threw pebbles down at them, faces would look up. Then you would wave at them. If the pebbles came too close, however, you would draw back out of sight as quickly as possible.

A most spectacular rooftop performance was that of throwing match bombs. By winding together a handful of wooden kitchen matches, heads down, and sticking a cardboard fin in between the wooden ends, a child had a missile that would burst into flame and smoke when it hit the sidewalk. This exhibition, with its element of bravado, was usually saved for that moment just before one retired from the roof.

It seemed less brazen or, at least, less dangerous to play pranks on timid servant girls; also, they could always be relied upon for the best response. Every household had a servant girl who began her day by sweeping the front stoop and then cleaning out the debris and dust that usually collected in the areaways. Just before noon she polished the outer glassed vestibule doors and shined the brasswork; then she disappeared from view into the vestibule to do the inner entrance doorknobs and the brass umbrella-stands.

If you looked over the back edge of the roof you could see the maze of grassed yards used for hanging laundry; they were criss-crossed with ropes and divided into rectangles by a continuous eight-foot fence. This yard fence was topped with a two-by-four which was excellent for "tight-rope-walking." Once I went the whole length of the Hamilton Terrace yards without falling off. I still recall the difficulty and embarrassment of trying to keep my balance while acknowledging neighbors who glowered from their back windows as I went by with arms outstretched.

From the rooftop you could also see all the way to Convent Avenue, where next to a massive Byzantine brownstone church there was an old white wooden building that we called "the country house." It had old-fashioned white balustrades all around the edge of its roof. I presumed that these were for safety in case anyone wished to walk on the rooftop, and I decided that when I was old enough to build my own home, I would have roof railings just like them. I remember taking pad and pencil to the roof and drawing a sketch of the country-house balustrade which I kept for many years as plans for the house that I someday would build.

There was one other white wooden country house like it, uptown on Washington Heights where I ventured by bicycle on special days. This white wooden house sat overlooking the Hudson River on a high wooded hill called Fort Washington Woods at Fort Tryon. The house commanded an almost unbeliev-

There was an old white house with roof balustrades.

able view, and I was sure that the owner, Mr. Billings, was just about the richest man in the world. Even his garage was magnificent: it had a big turntable in the floor so that one could drive in and have servants push the automobile around till it faced the entrance again. Some of the earlier cars of that time, it seems, had no reverse.

The Billings' chauffeurs were not very friendly, but I do remember an extraordinarily amiable man who lived and worked in a nearby house and who wore a gray smock and had clay on his hands. His name was George Gray Barnard. If I made the trip to Fort Washington Woods without seeing him about, I would bicycle idly around his place until he saw me. Then if I were lucky, he would come out and wave me over to visit him. He would leave his work (which seemed to be that of making very large statues) and, sitting on a marble bench in his garden with a glass of milk for me and a cup of tea for himself, he would tell me stories about the wooded area thereabouts. He often told me how General Washington and General Hamilton had engaged the British there, forcing them back to their ships in the Hudson. And he showed me a sketch he had made of Hamilton, from which he intended to create a statue. Once he showed me arrowheads and iron pots and ancient-looking hinges that he had dug from the garden.

The whole wooded heights were spotted with cellar holes dating back to Revolutionary days and with unexplainable excavations of feldspar and mica stonework. If you were lucky you could find sheets of mica which we called isinglass. I once found a sheet about the size of a large dinner plate which was so transparent that when I held it up I could see across the Hudson and pick out tiny houses on top of the Palisades in New Jersey. In one excavation I found a fine silver thimble, and when I rubbed away some of the encrusted dirt, there came to light the name "John Hancock." My excitement was great and I hurried home with my treasure buried deep in my pocket and covered with mica and other stone relics to keep it from falling out. That night when, preparing to show my find to my family, I cleaned away more of the dirt, I found the name "John Hancock" followed by the words "Insurance Company." My disappointment, however, was not as momentous or long-lasting as the thrill of possibly having found an important piece of Americana, and I suppose that excitement has lasted and perpetuated itself many times during my life.

Just before my last bicycle trip to Fort Washington Woods, the Billings house burned down, the magnificent garage was boarded up, and the grounds went unattended. This, however, allowed me to roam about the estate and even to explore the ruins of the old house. The entrance and front hallway were the only parts left intact; the upper floors were burned out. A charred banister railing curved upward with stairs that went to nowhere but the empty sky. Behind the stairway I found a small electric buzzer box for summoning servants to particular rooms. There were twenty-six rooms listed, and one room was that of "Young Master Billings." I have often wondered what became of Master Billings and if he knew the woods around his own home as well as I did.

Soon afterward, the collection of George Gray Barnard, the Billings' neighbor, grew to museum-sized proportions and became the nucleus of the Cloisters. An arched entrance tunnel of marble still climbs the cliff from Riverside Drive to where the Billings home once was, but the woods and the scenes of my early adventures are now completely lost in a parklike landscape with cement benches and chromium drinking fountains. Probably that time before the few remaining pieces of countryside were covered with the cement and apartment buildings of an overlapping city was the last period when a boy could discover a recognizable tie with the past of Manhattan Island. Now when I visit Washington Heights, I take pleasure in the privilege of having known it fifty years ago, and I realize that the thoughts I had about historic America have become persistent echoes that I can cherish.

The same richness that overtakes the big city also leaves it poverty stricken in lore, and the people usually have little or no knowledge of the past—or sadder still, the desire for such knowledge. The excavations that I explored on Fort Washington Heights are now beneath a great village of apartment buildings; buried, too, are some historic moments of General Washington and General Hamilton.

I have relived my New York boyhood adventures over again in many places: the backyards and brownstone steps, the trap-door to the roof, and the dark hallways of my childhood have been the theater for the haphazard pattern of a half century of recollections and dreams. And even now when I travel to the city, I often make a sentimental detour through those streets just for the pleasure of recapturing reassuring instances or sounds or thoughts that at one time were completely fresh and new.

Hamilton Terrace, when I saw it last spring, still had the flavor of my isolated world of remembrances, and I felt the urge and perhaps a longing need for the simple experience of stopping and walking in my own past. Feeling like an insistent ghost, I decided to enjoy that peculiar comfort found in the privilege of revisitation; I parked my car on Convent Avenue, outside the old white wooden country house I once knew, and embarked.

The white balustrades were gone. Even the whiteness of the old wooden house was gone. It had assumed the color and mood of extraordinary neglect. Three pale yellowish rectangles on one outer wall outlined long missing shutters. The upper porch railing was gone and six posts of the lower porch balustrade had been used to patch a gaping hole in the lattice underneath. Nine finely carved solid wooden columns showed evidence of having once been painted, before their grain had wrinkled into the solid pattern of surface rot. They held up a porch roof in equal disrepair. The porch steps shakily meandered downward into a grassless bit of lawn space adjacent to a row of overflowing garbage cans belonging to a recently built tenement house next door—not really next door, but with its brick shoulder leaning flush against the clapboards. The old house was suffering every indignity that the city could contrive.

To make the crowded scene more grotesque, a life-sized statue rose beside the dilapidated stairway and an imposing marble base explained in cut letters that this was the home of Alexander Hamilton. The bronze man, in knee pants and stockings, faced away from the ghostly building behind him and stared at the row of buildings across the way where several of the occupants had gathered to sit on the stone stoops and sun themselves. I continued to read the Gothic letters on the pedestal.

Webster had written: "He smote the rock of national resources and abundant streams of revenues gushed forth." Another facet of the pedestal proclaimed: "His rare powers entitled him to the fame of being the first intellectual product of America." And "The name of Hamilton would have honored Greece in the age of Aristides."

"Those are true words," said a voice. A smallish Negro man nodded a salutation and taking a rag from his pocket, he flicked some soot from the marble tablet. "The General was a fine man."

He spoke in a manner of greeting and I responded, "I've always wanted to

The old white wooden
Country House
once had Balustrades . . .

. . . now they were gone.

know more about Hamilton. You know, I once lived right around the corner from this house and never knew it was Hamilton's house."

"Yes," he said, "a lot of people have forgotten that this was Hamilton's house."

His face was a bit unlike the other Negroes of the neighborhood, the color of soft cordovan, and he wore a tiny patch of white beard on his lower lip that gave him a precise distinction. Beneath a much-used overcoat he wore the blue tick butler's apron of a houseman.

"When I lived in the neighborhood," I said, "this house was clean and white. But that was a long time ago. It looks as if it hasn't been painted for fifty years."

"About thirty-five years," corrected the man. "It had its last touching-up when the front was painted in June of 1933. I live here, you know."

That was how I met Raleigh Henry Daniels, the custodian and caretaker of The Grange. His apartment was in the basement, beneath which is a sub-basement. Above his dark hallways were the closed and vacant rooms of an eloquent past whose windows once looked out on lawns and towering trees; in winter, when the trees were bare, that view extended all the way to the New Jersey Palisades.

"The shutters are closed now," mused Mr. Daniels, "and I know that is the way the General would want it. He designed those triple hung windows for another kind of view." Mr. Daniels seldom referred to Alexander Hamilton as most people do. Sometimes it was just "Hamilton," which, he told me, was the name Mrs. Hamilton usually called her husband, but for the most part he referred to the legendary figure as "the General." There was a manner about Mr. Daniels which made one think that he was caretaker for Hamilton himself and I believe that secretly and perhaps profoundly he considered himself just that.

On my first meeting with Mr. Daniels I spent over an hour with him and only on my way back to Connecticut did I realize that my original purpose for stopping near Hamilton Terrace had been to visit my own childhood place. Since then my interest in personal nostalgia has become engulfed by the strange predicament of The Grange and a friendship with the lone occupant of that remarkable house. The determined but calm confusion of Hamilton's last days seems to live on in the history of The Grange, and Daniels has lived there patiently aware of the presence of a strange perplexity that haunts the

.. the bronze man faced away from the Ghostly building..

building. It must have been frustrating for him to know that the slightest repair or paint had to first await the consideration of the Department of the Interior, the National Park Service, building commissions, historians, and an overpowering variation of public opinion, while the building deteriorated. Mr. Daniels sometimes overstepped his authority by nailing down a loose board here or there. "They pop up as fast as I nail them down," he said, "the old wood doesn't hold the nails like it used to."

It has been almost a half century since a trust fund was set up for The Grange's maintenance, and years have now accumulated after an appropriation of nearly half a million dollars was granted for its restoration. One time when restoration and removal were completely decided upon, architects worked feverishly on the plans and in 1957 an expensive "200th-year Hamilton Anniversary" brochure was printed, announcing the great project and showing the artist's conception of how The Grange would soon look in its new location. The haunting spell of confusion persisted over The Grange, however, and the project was forgotten. The Grange, which has become much less a monument to Alexander Hamilton than to the mechanics of disharmony, according to neighborhood folklore, seems to have inherited the stigma of uncertainty from that moment when Hamilton turned his back on it and left for his fatal appointment with Aaron Burr.

An exquisite poignancy must have taken over the mind of Alexander Hamilton on that early morning in 1804. His departing look at this newly built house in which his wife and children were sleeping could not have been a hasty glance over his shoulder: he must have stopped and prayed, with his eyes open, that this might not be a last view. "The dueling ground was about two and a half hours away," Mr. Daniels told me, "and the General had to get a barge across the river. So I guess he left at sunrise in order to be there at seven. On July 11 in 1804 the sun rose at 4:34. The Grange must have looked beautiful to him at that moment." Mr. Daniels had taken the trouble to research the time of sunrise in an old almanac.

On my second visit to The Grange, Mr. Daniels was outside the house, raking the pitifully small bit of lawn space in front. "I thought I'd throw a bit of seed around," he said. "I guess they'll not mind my doing that. It's not the kind of grass the General likes, but it was the best I could buy around here. He likes red clover, you know." Actually I was unaware of what kind of grass the General liked, but in the process of research later, I learned that indeed Hamilton had a liking for red clover. ". . . the greatest part of my little farm (The Grange) will be dedicated to grass," he wrote to his friend Judge Richard Peters in 1798. "It has been mentioned to me that you have in your quarters a species of red clover, the stock of which is less coarse than ours and the quality very good. If this be so, and you think well of it, you will oblige me by procuring and sending me a couple of baskets of the seed."

"...the pitifully small lawnspace..." 1967

Another time Mr. Daniels commented upon the few shreds of hedge that remain around The Grange. "The General liked laurel best you know, and if they'd let me, I'd find some to plant around the place. He liked hyacinths and tulips and lilies too." It was only in the process of much reading that I learned Hamilton did have a fondness for laurel, and it was then that I began to wonder how Daniels knew so much about his General. There was, in fact, an eighteen-foot circle of wild roses and laurel, with seasonal plantings of lilies, tulips, and hyacinths directly in front of The Grange's entrance, but laurel dominated the planting. People passing by The Grange on any January 11 will see a wreath of laurel tied to the Hamilton statue. It is an old, much-used wreath. Mr. Daniels bought it a long while ago, and he has never forgotten Alexander Hamilton's birthday, after which the wreath has always been carefully cleaned and wrapped in cellophane until the next January 11.

Mr. Daniels would often correct me on historical and geographical points about the neighborhood, and as he came from St. Augustine, Florida, I always wondered where he had obtained his information. His library consisted of only a few books, but he was a quiet and most observing man and he had both the time and the quiet for observation. "The Grange is a sad house," he commented. "The sadness seems to have a special meaning; perhaps I am the only one aware of that. It is as if the General wants to say something across the years, and there is no one else to listen."

The statue in front of The Grange, he told me, was originally in front of the Hamilton Club in Brooklyn, and perhaps no one else would have noticed it but the bronze face then looked directly toward The Grange: now where the statue has been moved (outside the front entrance of The Grange), Hamilton stares toward the spot where he fell on that July morning in 1804. I suppose that Daniels has had the time to put together such fancy with fact for his own pleasure, which has resulted in his enjoying the otherwise solemn spell of the old house. But he was not superstitious. "Do you ever hear noises?" I once asked him, almost hoping that I might hear of some strange and ghostly incident. "Only before a storm," he said. "Then the old beams in the framework stiffen and groan. Sometimes there is a boom or a crackling in the upper rooms. But that is just the way they built these old houses, pinned together with pegs that let the beams stretch and breathe when the weather changes. If they used nails, the beams would have split. The General's father-in-law cut most of the beams and soaked them in water for two months before he shipped them down the river from his place at Albany, and he even sent down the wooden pegs. Some of the beams still show the up-and-down saw-cuts from General Schuyler's own saw-mill."

I saw these beams in the attic, and Mr. Daniels pointed out some others. "When they reached this part of the roof framing," he said, "they ran out of the good beams that General Schuyler had sent down from Albany, and they had to have other beams right away; so they tore down some of the old farmhouse that the General lived in while they were building The Grange. Here are those very beams—you can see by the now unused mortices that they had been used in another building at one time." Mr. Daniels' eyes showed a twinkle of pleasure at his detective work.

Like most other houses in the vicinity, my old home, a brownstone on Hamilton Terrace, is now occupied by a Negro family, and in discussing the local population, I once asked Mr. Daniels, "When did Harlem start to overflow into Washington Heights?" I should have known better than to think of the New York Negro population as "Harlem."

"Why you're in Harlem right now," he said. "The real Washington Heights is quite a way uptown overlooking the Hudson River. Washington Heights is just what the white folks called this area about a century ago when they wanted to divide themselves from the colored folk who began settling in the Harlem valley. Now that the colored folk are moving in here, maybe people will begin calling it Harlem again. That's what the General called it, you know. He called The Grange his 'Harlem country place.' I think he'd be pleased to know that the colored folk are beginning to live around his house now. He liked us, you know."

Actually there is too little known of Hamilton's personal feelings about the Negro, because his deep respect for the race was not a quality that many of his followers chose to applaud him for. Even the Emancipation Society did "more talking than acting" for Hamilton's liking, and repeatedly he demanded that "in token of our sincerity, let us free all of our slaves at once." On one occasion he is said to have bought a slave for the sole purpose of freeing him. Hamilton's West Indian past, however, led some of his tormentors to "wonder whether he was really against slavery or just for Negroes." Negroes of present-day New York have a remarkable understanding of Hamilton's attitude, and his statue on Convent Avenue has a special significance to them. "It sure is a shame about that nice man's house," said one passerby as he saw me making a sketch of it. "He was good to us. I wish we could do something about fixing his house up, neat-like, so it wouldn't be such an eyesore to our neighborhood."

"If this was the house of one of our patriots," said one Puerto Rican who stopped to watch over my shoulder, "we would tear down that apartment house and we would plant gardens all around. It is sad," he added, "to see how little the Americans have in their hearts for their great past."

I had to agree. "It's a poor example," I said, "but perhaps we'll get some gardens around here some day."

In the hour or two that I sat sketching the building, many other people stopped to watch, and each one felt called upon to comment on the frightful condition of the house. Students on their way to the nearby College of the City of New York seemed outraged when they spoke out. "I'll bet that building is the only National Monument in America that doesn't fly the American flag!" said one.

Being a good caretaker, Mr. Daniels did not dare to leave his Grange for long, but when the weather was good, he would sometimes "walk around the General's estate" after supper. He carried a cane said to have been made from one of the thirteen gum trees planted by Hamilton himself. Knowing just about where The Grange's old boundaries were, Mr. Daniels would stroll east to Hamilton Terrace, then after a slight detour at an apartment house—the Hamilton barn once stood there—he would walk to 145th Street, and westward to busy Amsterdam Avenue. At 141st Street he finally turned eastward and home to The Grange. Sometimes he did not go inside immediately, but sat a while on the porch. Nodding toward the statue, he once told me with a chuckle, "The General and I like to see the sun go down." I had the feeling that the chuckle was to cover his embarrassment at actually being serious.

In reconsidering, however, I found Mr. Daniels too thoughtful and honest a man to be embarrassed about his reverence for General Hamilton. One night as I finished a stroll around the old Grange boundaries with Mr. Daniels and then saw him back to his little apartment in the cellar, I stopped outside long enough to see his light go on. Above, the street light made distinguishable a sign that Mr. Daniels had nailed to the main entrance door, "CLOSED UNTIL FURTHER NOTICE." The old house loomed black and dejected. It was I who felt embarrassed.

This was the last time that I saw Mr. Daniels during my research on The Grange, for then I buried myself in the business of writing. When my writing was finished, I brought it up for Mr. Daniels to read. He was being measured for a sort of museum guard suit. The rotting porch was being rebuilt and there was a sign on a board across the steps, "SOON TO BE OPENED TO THE PUBLIC."

"I think maybe they're really going to do something now," he said.

I remembered how such plans had been made ten years ago. "At least they are going to clean up the old place," I said, "and you're going to get that coat of paint on The Grange."

"I guess my prayers are being answered," he said simply.

I do not know what eventual restoration and relocation is in store for The Grange. After having researched its history and seen it in my mind's eye so vividly, I find it almost disappointing to look in upon the rooms now. The scale appears smaller than it should be, as it often happens when things have been neglected for a long while. But Raleigh Henry Daniels to me shall never diminish. He represents a reverence and respect for a brilliant past and a deserving man. Hamilton's "rare powers," as the marble pedestal reads, "entitled him to the fame of being the first intellectual product of America." And no one has believed that more than Mr. Daniels.

The foregoing pages describe The Grange as it was when this book was started, early in 1967. By the end of the year, when the manuscript was completed, things had begun to happen. The Grange had received its first coat of paint in thirty-five years. It was a restorer's nightmare: one miserable, unauthentic coat of enamel was hurriedly slapped over unprepared, rotting wood, and a bilious brown covered the porch floors. The paint was brushed over protruding nails and mistakenly over the leaded mullions of old windows. Where decorative eave moldings were missing—and a piece of tin substituted—that too was covered with enamel. But at least things had begun to happen, and The Grange was losing its haunted appearance. Hamilton's statue was cleaned. After nearly a half century of neglect, the stairs and bannisters had been repaired, with missing pieces added.

By the time this book went to press, The Grange was open to the public, although inside walls were still broken, with bricks showing through, and some of the ceilings were still shattered and fallen. Guides nevertheless were on hand to show visitors from one empty and dismal room to another. At first I thought that the philosophy of pleasing decay might have been the object of this strange exhibition, but that thought was dispelled by a bright red carpet with aluminum edging that covered much of the unrestored floors.

"Why is this open to the public?" I asked a uniformed guide.

"People want to see it," he replied. "And we do want to explain why we haven't been able to do more, why everything must wait until the house is moved. We are working on that, too."

"But Alexander Hamilton would certainly have had better taste than to open his home in such a miserable state to visitors. What has happened to the original furniture?" I asked.

"We do have one piece here," the attendant said, directing me to the old dining room. "It really isn't an original Grange piece, but it *is* of the period."

He showed me a long curved dining-room sideboard with lion's claw legs and lion-head hardware typical of British furniture of the early to middle 1800s. Above, a large portion of the ceiling had fallen and a piece of sheetrock had been nailed over the hole. The Grange, I thought to myself, is still haunted. The spell of confusion and uncertainty has never left it.

Perhaps hours or months or years after this book has been published The Grange will emerge from its predicament. The problems of moving an ancient building, of vacating land and demolishing buildings for such a project might be overcome, and The Grange may finally sit upon an appropriate piece of land with grass and trees. But the thought continually returns to me that there should be a park or piece of natural countryside in every city where historic buildings might be moved to. All over the nation are meaningful examples of early buildings that must either be moved or destroyed because of highways or new building projects. Now and then a well-meaning historic society will "save the old landmark" and mark it with a plaque. But most often this effort only ridicules the old house by making it appear grotesque and at its worst, hemmed in between modern buildings or flanked by gas stations and badly designed office buildings. If only there were a piece of the original countryside left empty and waiting for such treasures.

In New York, Riverside Drive might have been kept intact, with its trees and grass and footpaths, for such historic treasures as The Grange. Within a century Riverside Drive would be a two or three mile-long park of historic sites, a sort of open-air museum of Americana.

"Right on the Hudson River," mused Mr. Daniels, "is where the General really wanted to build The Grange. It would have been respectful to him if they had moved it there. But people don't think nowadays. Except about themselves."

Maybe this thought will be reason enough for this book. If cities throughout America will consider keeping tracts of land reserved for historic buildings, the plight of The Grange will not have been in vain.

Eric Sloane
Cornwall Bridge
Connecticut

Sketches from the Research Notebook

The Grange is one of the least documented of historical buildings, and the little scraps of early information that can be pieced together often contradict one another. Therefore the following sketches are contrived, to the best of my ability, to show my own interpretation of how The Grange and The Grange property evolved from the time of Hamilton. *Eric Sloane*

No historical landmark seems to have been neglected as much as The Grange. I could not unearth any Grange maps, much less any of the first land maps and surveys, in the libraries or private collections. But from other maps and information I have sketched in my findings and added my own interpretations, which I believe to be correct.

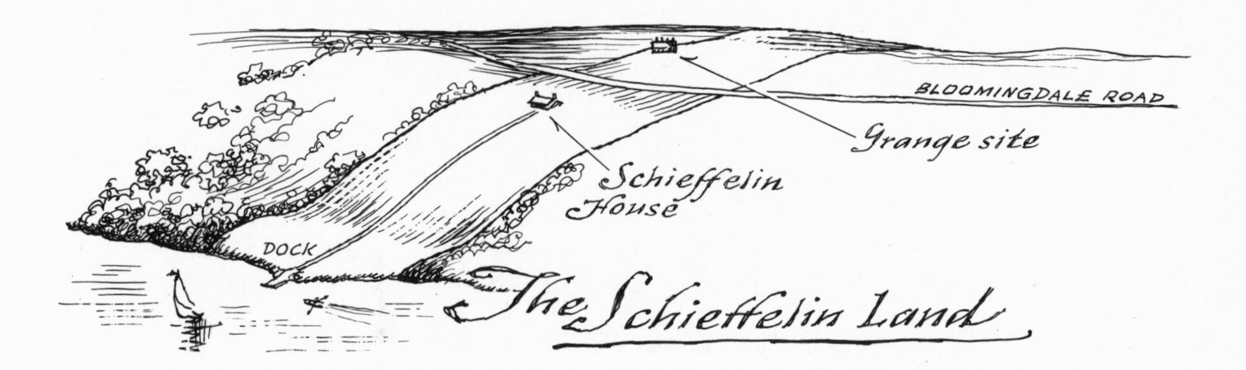

The Schieffelin Land

Washington had chosen Hamilton as his military strategist for Harlem Heights because of his familiarity with the countryside. Hamilton had often been bird shooting along the bank of the Hudson, and he had hunted all through the Harlem Valley, to the east. When Hamilton landed his boat during fishing jaunts, he used a small dock that extended from a stone abutment on the land of Jacob Schieffelin. Schieffelin had built a summer home on the hilltop just west of Bloomingdale Road, which led to New York City, then centered in lower Manhattan. The view of the Hudson from this estate had always intrigued Hamilton, and it became his hope that Schieffelin might sell it to him. But Schieffelin was in love with the estate too, and after some negotiation decided to sell only that part of the land east of Bloomingdale Road that was situated on a slight rise. You still could see the Hudson, but the main view was of the Harlem Valley. It was on this land and on that rise that Hamilton began to build The Grange, as shown by the dotted outline in the drawing below

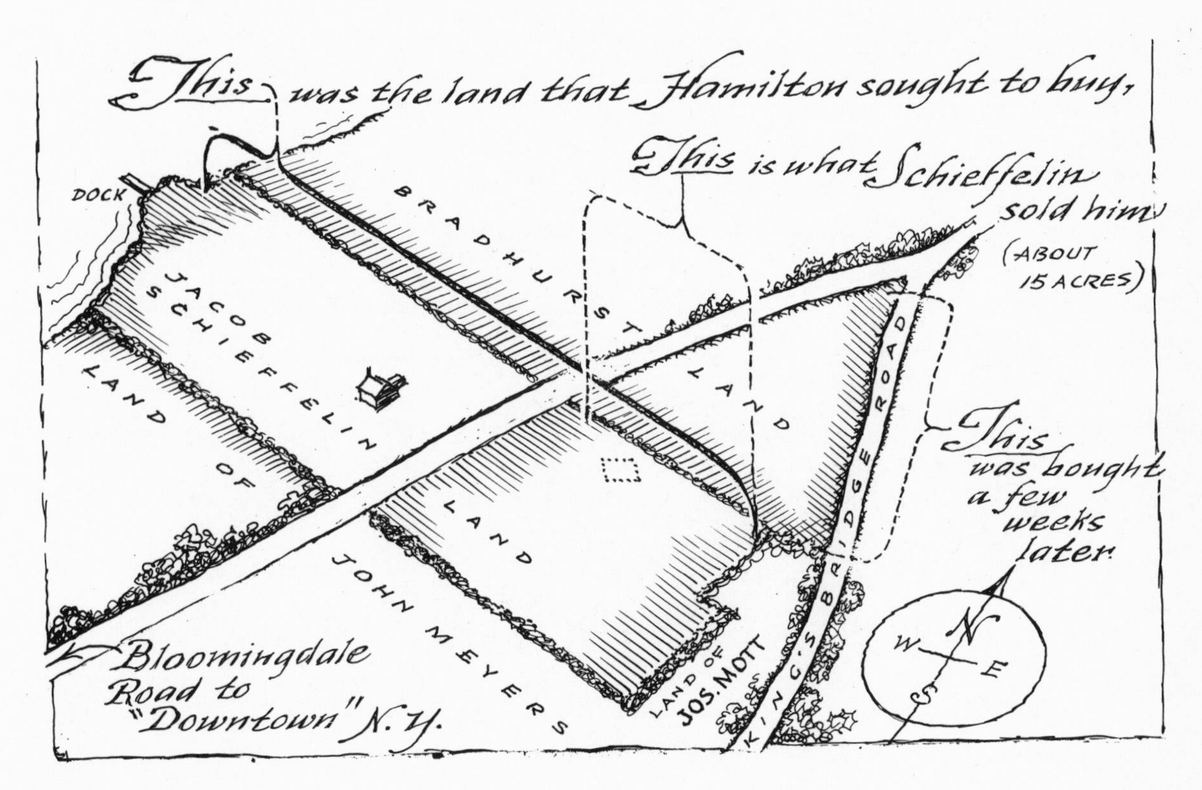

Opposite I have sketched my own interpretation of the early Grange boundaries and features. Hamilton had used a small cottage for summer holidays, very close to where he eventually built The Grange. Most historians think it was located at (A), but I believe that it stood at the dot indicated by (X). My reasoning is that there must have been a small farmhouse in conjunction with the barns, ice pond, etc., that were already on the Samuel Bradhurst triangle; also, since this small summer house was sometimes referred to as "the north cottage," it must have been north, not west, of The Grange.

(B) shows where The Grange was built, on a rocky shoulder of ground that lifted the building upward to gain a proper view of both the Hudson River and the Harlem Valley. (C) shows a complex of sheds and one barn already existing, and an icehouse that was rebuilt by Hamilton after The Grange was completed. (D) shows thirteen gum trees planted by Hamilton. (E) indicates where Tenth Avenue (now Amsterdam Avenue) was later placed. This was the first modern north-south avenue in Manhattan. Bloomingdale Road from Amsterdam Avenue southwestward still exists as Hamilton Place. (F) shows a brook that ran under Bloomingdale Road and through the triangular plot sold by Bradhurst to Hamilton, flowing into a ditch near the King's Bridge Road (now roughly St. Nicholas Avenue). (G) indicates a favorite after-dinner walk Hamilton often took around his estate: going from the front entrance eastward past the gum trees, he walked along the top of a bluff (now Hamilton Terrace) and northward through his complex of farm buildings. The walk continued past the icehouse and pond, then back to the rear-porch entrance of The Grange.

The division line between the original Schieffelin purchase and the later Bradhurst triangular purchase is about the middle of present-day 144th Street. (H) among the trees of the lower sketch is where The Grange was moved to and still stands—next to St. Luke's Episcopal Church—at this writing adjacent to 141st Street and to the land of the College of the City of New York

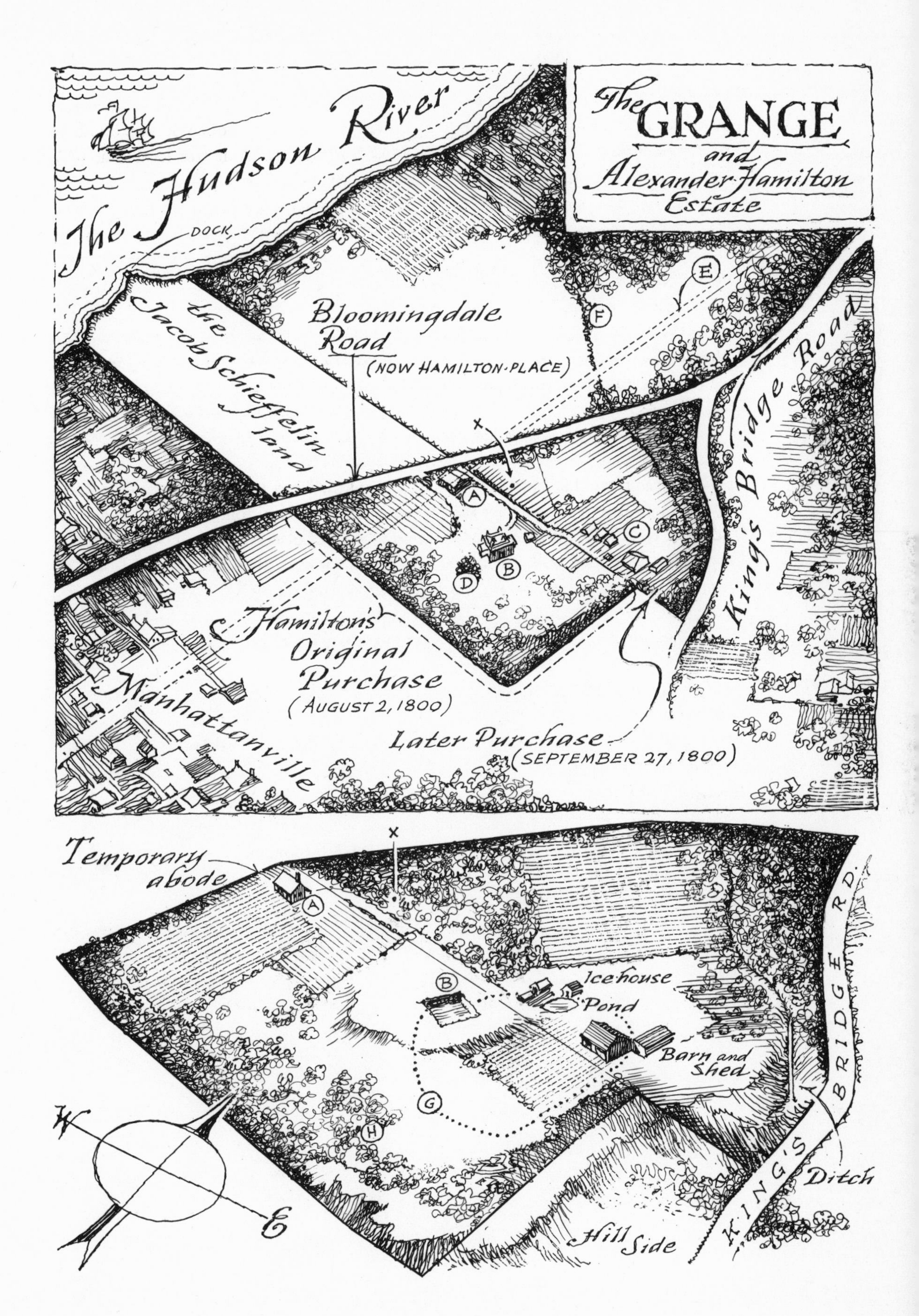

The GRANGE
and
Alexander Hamilton
Estate
The Hudson River
DOCK
the Jacob Schieffelin land
Bloomingdale Road
(NOW HAMILTON·PLACE)
King's Bridge Road
Hamilton's Original Purchase
(AUGUST 2, 1800)
Manhattanville
Later Purchase
(SEPTEMBER 27, 1800)
A
B
C
D
E
F
Temporary abode
A
B
Ice house
Pond
Barn and Shed
G
H
KING'S BRIDGE RD.
Ditch
Hill Side
W
E

When the American eagle was voted the "national emblem," there were also plans for designating a "national tree." Because the American sweet gum tree has a five-pointed starlike leaf and a particularly bright autumn foliage, during the late 1700s it was nearly voted our national tree. That, goes the legend, was the reason Hamilton planted thirteen gum trees, representing the original thirteen states, outside his study, intending them to be the center of a garden.

After Hamilton died the thirteen trees attracted more interest than did The Grange. People went to see the trees, artists painted them. Yet prints or paintings of The Grange itself are remarkably rare. Century-old writings about The Grange dwell only upon the sad condition of the building. Even after The Grange had been moved, the thirteen trees were carefully fenced and there was an effort to build a small park around them; but the new streets and building excavations caused them to die suddenly, and the project was abandoned.

At the turn of the century land in Harlem became tremendously valuable and many ancient landmarks were lost. Sometimes the location of an old landmark would coincide with the new east, west, north, south street plans for modern Manhattan, and these happy accidents saved a few historic houses. But The Grange was found to be askew and projecting into the middle of what would soon be 143rd Street. Obviously, it would have to be turned, moved, or completely destroyed. It should have been left intact, of course, and made the center of an Alexander Hamilton Park, but people were too busy at that time making profits with their land to think about historic landmarks.

When The Grange was moved in 1889, the thirteen gum trees, before they died, had become eighty-seven-year-old giants. The lower sketch shows The Grange just after it was moved across a dirt lane, which is now Convent Avenue. The view is from the approximate position of Alexander Hamilton's study in The Grange before the building had been moved

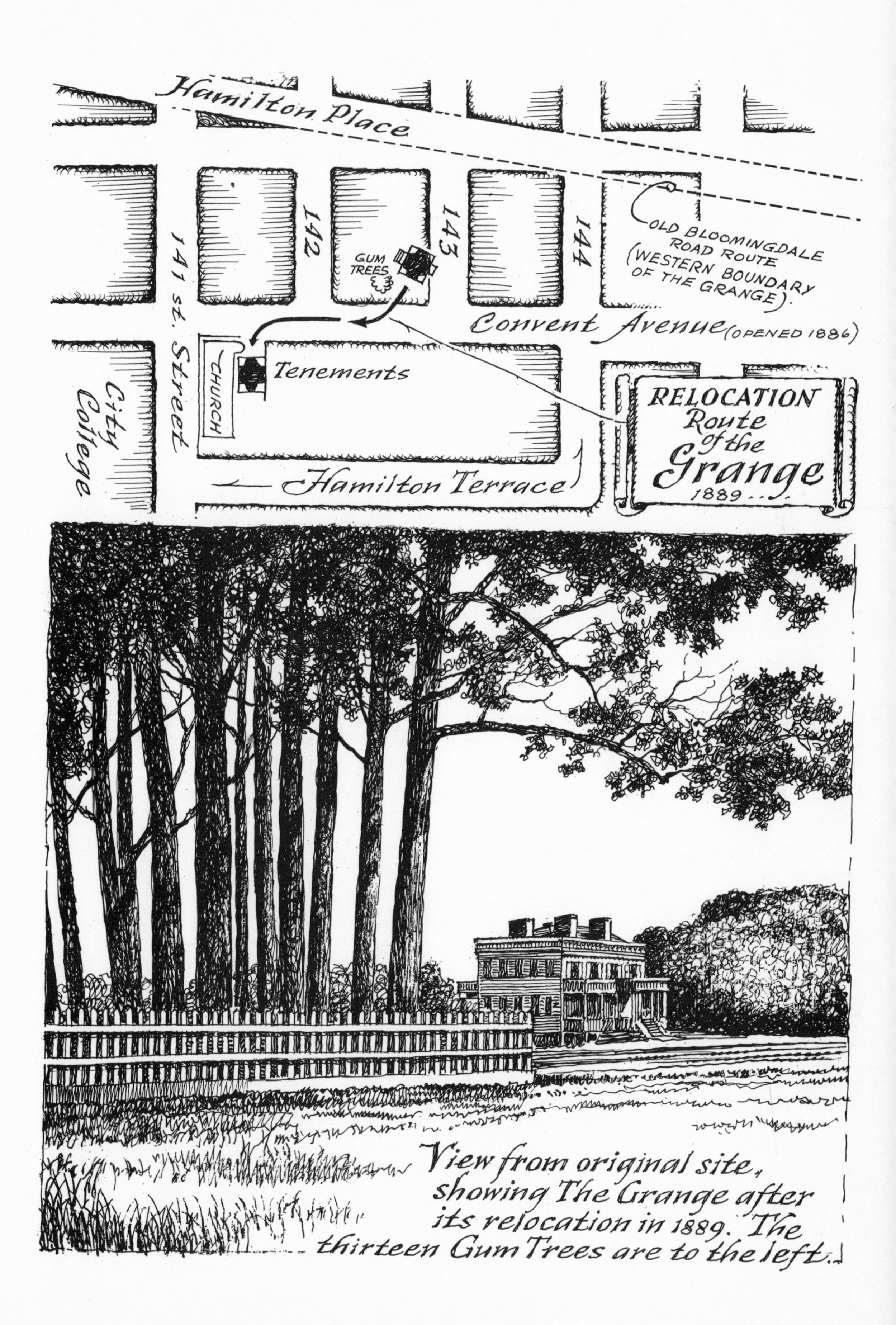

View from original site, showing The Grange after its relocation in 1889. The thirteen Gum Trees are to the left.

Apple trees were planted along the eastern bluff, with evidence of a proposed terrace (where Hamilton Terrace now stands). Reconstructing this scene in my mind, I imagine this terrace was a favorite for the General's evening walks. "There is rest and reflection in an eastern view," he said.

It was not the lively western view he had hoped for, but Hamilton was a man who contended well with disappointments. Though he built The Grange on an elevation and then lifted it on high foundations, there was still not his longed-for view of the Hudson, so he concentrated on the Harlem Valley to the east. His bedroom, his study, the gum trees, and the terrace all overlooked this eastern view.

"And when they moved The Grange," Daniels remarked, "they moved it to the east near his terrace, where the General used to stroll and view the Valley and the King's Bridge Road below"

The Grange c.1890
MOVED and READY FOR THE CHURCH TO BE BUILT AGAINST IT.

There is no actual record of The Grange basement layout, but here is my idea of the arrangement, as gleaned from old manuscripts and descriptions. There was a double crane fireplace (for cooking) on one side of the kitchen, a three-hole stew stove on the other side. The compartment marked (X) is the logical place for a dumbwaiter to connect to the dining room above. This is not mentioned in any record but there could be no other way for meals to have been served without a long and improbable walk to the stairs.

The "store room" was just that during later years when The Grange was occupied by other families, but I presume that this room was originally a servant's or caretaker's room. It was directly beneath the General's study. The "family dining room" was used when the house was just opened for the warmer months and when there were no guests; its big fireplace and low ceilings provided adequate and quick warmth. Servants then dined in the ironing room or in the kitchen

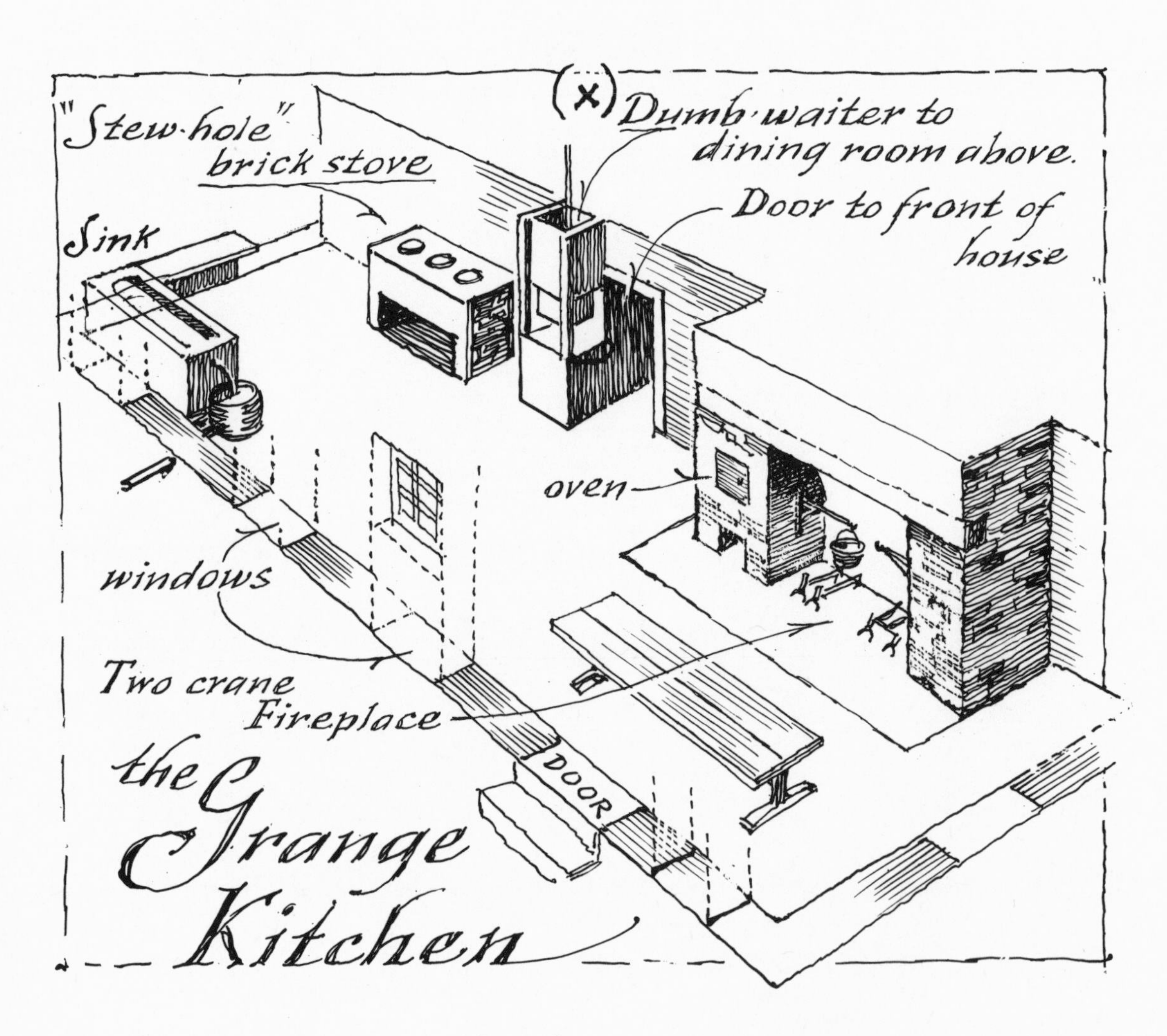

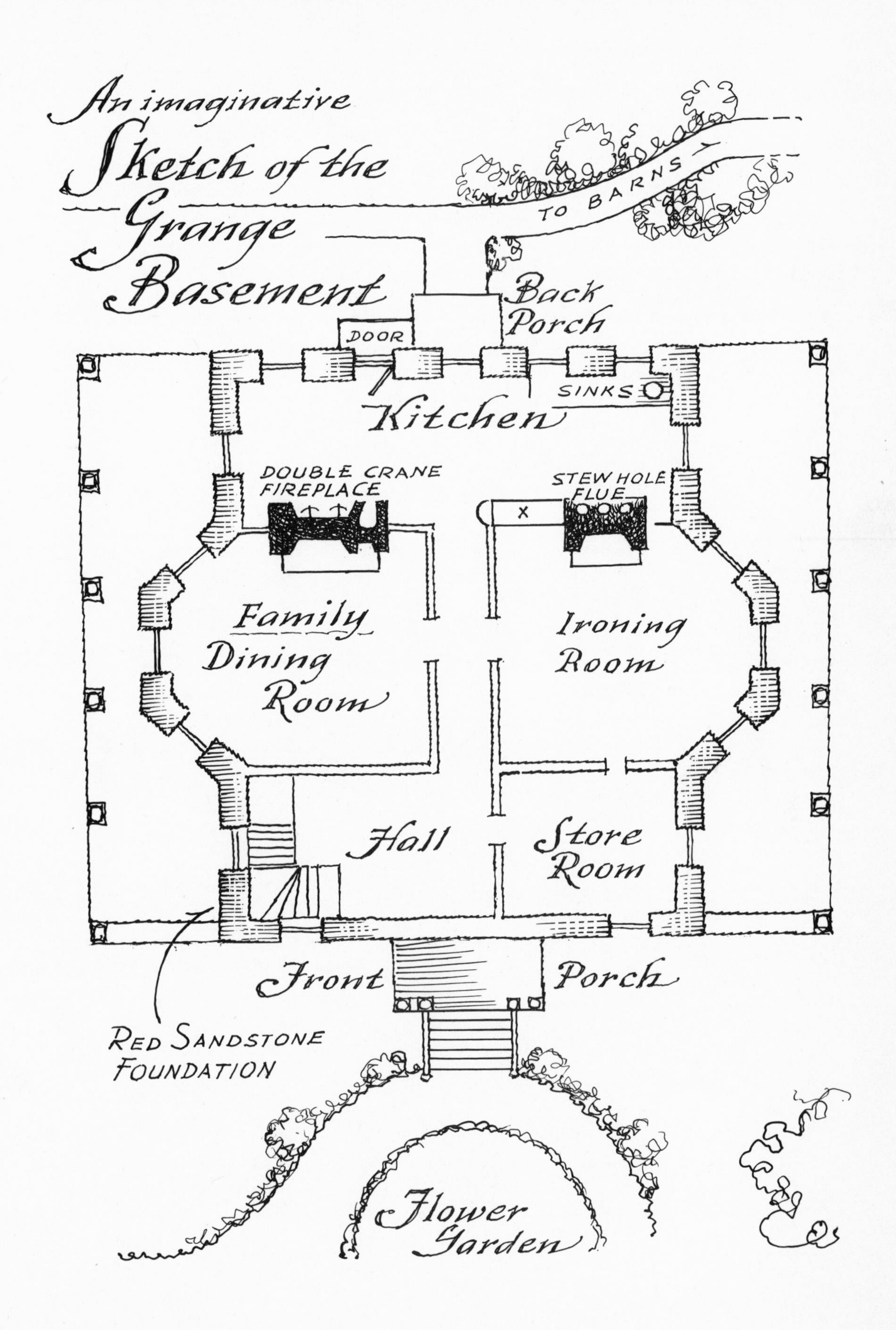
An imaginative
Sketch of the
Grange
Basement
TO BARNS
Back
Porch
DOOR
SINKS
Kitchen
DOUBLE CRANE
FIREPLACE
STEW HOLE
FLUE
X
Family
Dining
Room
Ironing
Room
Hall
Store
Room
Front
Porch
RED SANDSTONE
FOUNDATION
Flower
Garden

The symmetrical purity of The Grange's design is shown best in this first-floor plan. Like a mathematical equation arranged to equal a perfect formula for the General's summer entertaining, the properly placed study, or library, adjacent to the entrance hall (with a view of those entering the house), the arched entrance to both parlor and dining room, and the matching guest rooms at the back all result in a small architectural triumph.

The whole arrangement is held together by the twin-octagon theme, which supports the house both aesthetically and architecturally. These two octagonal rooms make the most of the two views, one toward the Hudson and the other over the Harlem Valley; three triple-hung room-high windows make an arc of these two separate panoramic views, and reflecting mirrors once gave the effect of complete openness. These two rooms for entertaining sound the note and reason for The Grange's existence.

The compartment marked (X) is the most probable location for a dumbwaiter.

The two views were each given their own piazza. The General's study gave him a view to the east and also of the gum trees he had planted (shown in the lower right)

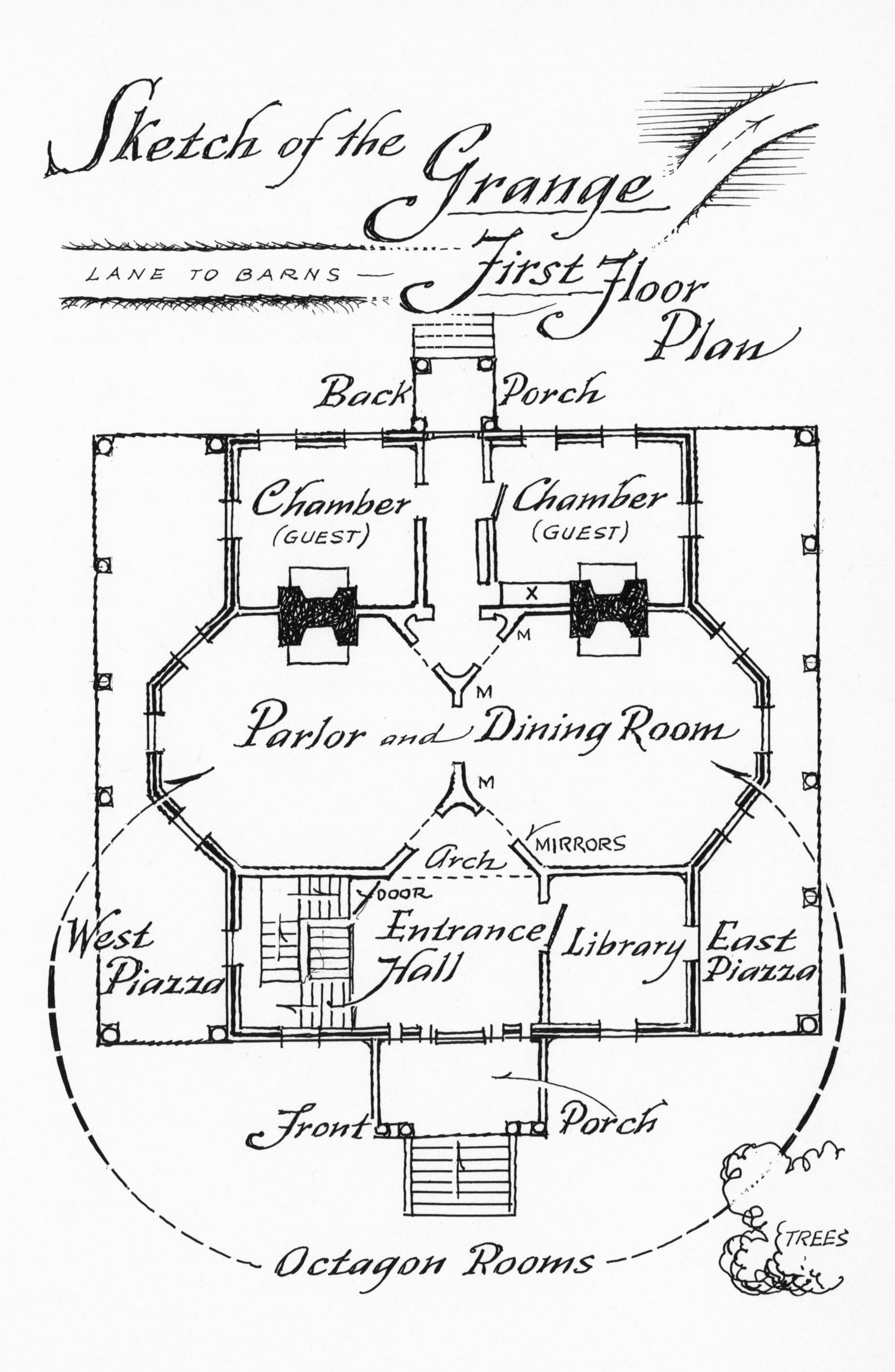
Sketch of the Grange
First Floor Plan
LANE TO BARNS
Back Porch
Chamber (GUEST)
Chamber (GUEST)
X
M
M
Parlor and Dining Room
M
MIRRORS
Arch
DOOR
West Piazza
Entrance Hall
Library
East Piazza
Front Porch
TREES
Octagon Rooms

Researchers have placed the Hamiltons, their children, and guests in almost every bedroom of The Grange, but after much thought I would like to offer my own opinion. Opposite, I have drawn a sketch of the second floor of the building and have given the bedrooms numbers.

The researchers have called that long small room (marked (X) in my drawing) "the only closet in The Grange." It seems a strange oversight, they insist, that "The Grange was unequipped with suitable clothes closets." The truth is simple: *there were no clothes closets in the 1700s.* The word "closet," as a matter of fact, meant a very private apartment or conference room, according to dictionaries of the day, and not a place for hanging or storing apparel. Clothes, at the time of The Grange's building, were hung from wall pegs, or were stored in chests and furniture drawers. The clothes closet, as we know it, did not appear until the mid 1800s.

Therefore, I believe that Bedroom 1 was Mrs. Hamilton's room, with the long closetlike compartment as that lady's private dressing room. I believe that Bedroom 2 (opposite Mrs. Hamilton's room) was the General's bedroom, except when there was a very special guest; on such an occasion the General would join his wife in her room and offer his own room to the guest. Indeed, guests have stayed in Bedroom 2, and there is record of how the General stepped across the hall on one stormy night to ascertain the comfort of his guest.

Bedroom 3 originally had the attic stairs, which now cut into the "General's room," and it is my opinion that this was the boys' room.

The Family Living Room, which stretched across the whole rear of the second floor, was furnished for the relaxation and comfort of the family. No doubt there were musical instruments here, and it is hinted that the girls sometimes used one end as sleeping quarters, perhaps set apart by portable screens. The two fireplaces made this very probable.

As beautifully as the first floor was designed for formal and country entertainment, the second floor was arranged for the quiet and comfort of the family

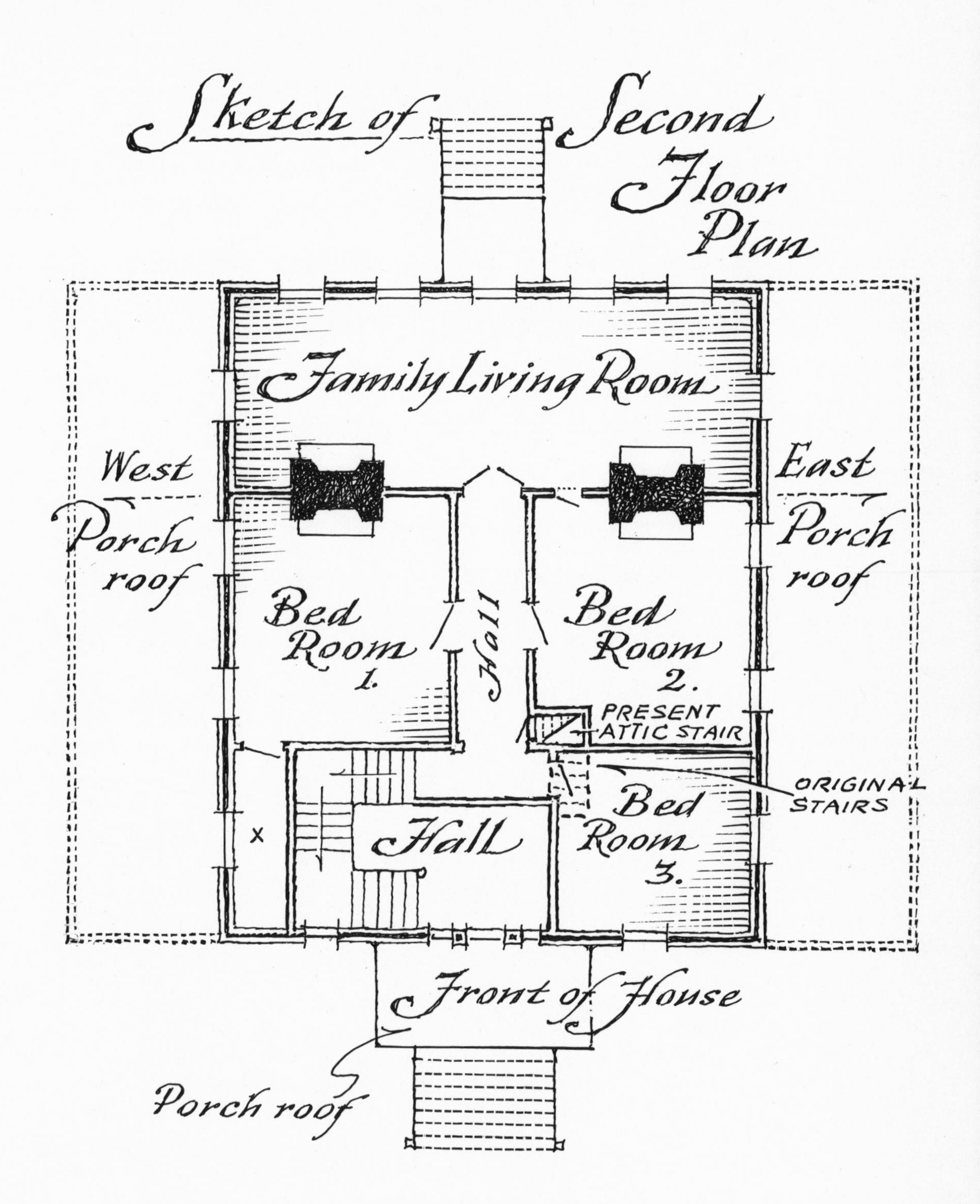
Sketch of Second Floor Plan
Family Living Room
West Porch roof
East Porch roof
Bed Room 1.
Hall
Bed Room 2.
PRESENT ATTIC STAIR
ORIGINAL STAIRS
Bed Room 3.
Hall
Front of House
Porch roof

The GRANGE

by Edward Anthony

Two photographs of a mahogany traveling desk used by Alexander Hamilton. Top picture shows desk ready for use; lower one shows how the desk looked when it was placed aboard a stagecoach or Hamilton's carriage for one of his numerous trips (except, of course, that the drawer at right would have been closed). *Allan McLane Hamilton Collection. U. S. National Museum*

The GRANGE

Seated at his mahogany traveling desk in a Philadelphia hotel, Alexander Hamilton in November, 1798, wrote to his wife, Elizabeth Schuyler Hamilton:

"I have formed a sweet project, of which I will make you my confidant, when I come to New York, and in which I rely that you will cooperate with me cheerfully.

"You may guess and guess and guess again,

"Your guessing will be still in vain.

"But you will not be the less pleased when you come to understand and realize the scheme."

This was Hamilton's first mention of his plans for the acquisition of land on which he was to build a country house.

The undertaking was an ambitious one. The site Hamilton had selected was approximately nine miles from the town house the Hamiltons occupied in lower Manhattan.

The house would be built in an area considered by some to be outside the limits of New York City proper, and known to many as Manhattanville. Today that section is miles south of the northernmost limits of the city—a little north of Convent Avenue and 141st Street, and only about a half hour by subway from where Hamilton lived downtown.

It is easy to understand Hamilton's desire to establish a home of his own. He and his family had been lower Manhattan nomads, moving from house to house in an effort to find something suitable for a growing family at a rental within his means. If the number of downtown dwellings the Hamiltons occupied during the comparatively few years when the addresses are traceable can be considered a criterion, it is not to much to assume that they moved ten or more times.

Hamilton never showed the slightest interest in building or buying a house in lower Manhattan, for reasons that will become apparent.

Events prior to and during the building of the Hamilton country home make it desirable, if not wholly essential, to determine when the Hamiltons lived at exactly what location. The New York City directories for the late 1700s and early 1800s were serviceable but understandably rudimentary. There were many errors of commission and omission. Moreover, often a family did not occupy a dwelling long enough—and this could easily have applied to the Hamiltons—to become listed.

We do know that in 1801 Hamilton's residence was given as 107 Liberty Street; in 1802 and 1803 it was 58 Partition Street, a thoroughfare that took in part of today's Fulton Street. The Hamilton address was 12 Garden Street in 1804. Just when Partition and Garden Streets disappeared cannot be determined but apparently it happened many years ago. Meyer Berger, the famous *New York Times* reporter who knew Manhattan history as few people did, stated in his "About New York" column in 1940 that he had visited "the ancient brick structure at 173 Cherry Street" which he identified as "the old Alexander Hamilton house, which stands under Manhattan Bridge among blackened tenements. Tugs and other deep-throated harbor craft bellow right into the backyard." The records of the New York Public Library reveal that there was also a Pine Street residence.

In *The Epic of New York City,* Edward Robb Ellis described George Washington's inauguration on April 30, 1789, when New York was the capital of the United States: "The chief notables led Washington out of the Senate Chamber onto the balcony (of Federal Hall) fronting on Wall Street. . . . Alexander Hamilton watched from a window of his home at 33 Wall Street." Therefore we now have six downtown home addresses for Hamilton. He was known to have had a Wall Street office, and it is possible that at one time he had a home there which also served as an office. Old newspaper clippings refer to a "No. 24" Broadway residence, which would make seven. Of course, Cherry Street may have once been known as Garden Street, but one can only guess at that.

Since moving from rented house to rented house was undoubtedly a wearing experience, the gypsying Hamiltons must have regarded their plan to build a home of their own as an exciting undertaking, one of the major events of their lives.

In 1798 one had to have the spirit of adventure to consider building a country house in the Manhattanville area, which was so distant from lower Manhattan. There was a stagecoach that ran from Bowling Green to 42nd Street—where Upper Manhattan began in those days—but it made the trip only three times a week, and beyond that point there was not much local service. As it was difficult to make a profit on short-haul transportation, New Yorkers either walked or provided their own conveyances.

The families who had settled in what was then regarded as an "outlying district" were motivated largely by the consideration that this early version of suburbia was healthful. Most of these people, alarmed by the prevalence of yellow fever and other contagious diseases in lower and upper Manhattan, had chosen this area because it had had none of the epidemics that had hit what was then regarded as "the heart of New York."

Most families capable of establishing a country seat owned one or more carriages and several horses and therefore had no transportation problem. Even those who had their own equipage sometimes preferred to make the trip by public conveyance. The only way to do this was to make application to Potter, Hyatt & Company's "New-York and Albany Mail Stage." The advertisements (which always hyphenated New York) announced: "For seats apply to William Vandervoort, No. 48, corner of Courtland and Greenwich streets, New-York." The stagecoach company naturally favored passengers who booked passage for the whole journey to Albany. The three-day trip cost 8 dollars, in addition to which Potter, Hyatt received a commission on the stopovers at Peekskill and Rhinebeck.

Hamilton's prominence undoubtedly made it easier for him to get a seat than the ordinary person, and some of the Hamilton biographies mention his visiting the site of his future country home by the Albany stage.

Three years had elapsed since Hamilton had resigned as Secretary of the Treasury. He would have liked to continue in Washington's cabinet, but the demands of a growing family were such that he found it increasingly difficult to meet his obligations on a salary of $3,000 a year.

Even Hamilton's critics—and he had many—did not challenge his patriotism. His career as Secretary of the Treasury was unavoidably a stormy one. When he took office as President Washington's first cabinet appointee, the new government of the United States of America had a back-breaking burden of debt, very little income, and practically no credit.

It has been written more than once that after six years as Secretary of the Treasury, during which he was frequently attacked by the press and an antagonistic minority in Congress, Hamilton found himself thinking fondly of leaving government service and pursuing a career that did not involve an almost daily battle to sell his ideas.

When he announced his intention to acquire the land on which to build a country house, some of his friends, knowing that he was still nursing political wounds, assumed that his urge to establish a rural retreat was one more manifestation of his withdrawal from the national scene. The desire to retire from public life was indeed real, but Hamilton, in resigning his cabinet post, assured a few intimates that if his country ever needed his services again, perhaps in some emergency requiring his particular type of experience, he would be glad to serve. He had enjoyed his cabinet post despite the headaches it entailed. No one relished a good political battle more than he and if he had been a man of means it is not too much to assume that he would have continued.

Hamilton was forty-one when he made the decision to build his country house, which he named in honor of the ancestral seat of his family in Scotland. His father, James Hamilton, had been the fourth son of Alexander Hamilton, of The Grange, Ayrshire.

As Hamilton began formulating his plans for the New York version of The Grange he could reflect on many accomplishments: as Secretary of the Treasury he had won the fight for the establishment of a Bank of the United States; he had contributed handsomely to confounding the skeptics who dismissed the Constitution as a mere piece of paper that could not be made to function; by funding the Colonial debt he had given the country the excellent credit that enabled trade and industry to flourish; and it was he who secured the establishment of a mint. Earlier, and this was his greatest achievement, he had been a powerful factor in the struggle for the adoption of the Constitution.

He had served in 1776 as captain of an artillery company, taking part in the actions on Harlem Heights and Long Island, at White Plains, and at Princeton and Trenton. He won the favorable notice of Washington and was made secretary and aide-de-camp to the general. For four years he handled most of Washington's correspondence, drafted many of his papers, made reports that were of great value to his chief on the condition of the army, including proposals for re-organizing and improving it. So the future master of The Grange could take satisfaction in having served his country, at a considerable sacrifice, before turning country gentleman.

Hamilton had written when The Grange was becoming a reality, "To men who have been so much harassed in the base world as myself, it is natural to look forward to complete retirement . . . as a perfect desideratum. This desire I have felt in the strongest manner, and to prepare for it has latterly been a favourite object. I thought I might not only expect to accomplish the object, but might reasonably aim at it and pursue the preparatory measures."

Commenting on the foregoing, Allan McLane Hamilton, a grandson of Alexander Hamilton, wrote, "It is true that these sentiments were directly provoked by his political disappointments, as well as a realization that he must make provision for his old age, but it may be assumed that the time had come for the enjoyment of the company of a house of his own in the quiet country. Possibly his familiarity with Vergil's bucolics, and especially the First Eclogue, had filled his mind with sylvan longings; or, again, there may have been the influence of his early life,—his birthplace being Nevis, one of the picturesque Antilles Islands which the British colonized in 1728—spent in a clime full of beauty and restfulness, that prompted him to look about for a retreat which was far enough removed from the bustle and affairs of men to enable him to find relaxation in the happiness of seclusion."

One of the harassments "in the base world" to which Allan Hamilton alluded was the harsh treatment the first Secretary of the Treasury received from enemies in Congress and hostile newspaper editors who, he thought, had misunderstood his motives in prevailing on Washington, during the Whisky Rebellion, to issue a statement declaring that the law would be enforced even if it were necessary to exercise all his Constitutional powers. The insurgents backed down and agreed to pay the tax. Hamilton considered the firm stand he urged to be one of his most important recommendations to the first President. The action taken demonstrated the ability of the Federal government to enforce the law of the land.

As much as Hamilton enjoyed a good scrap, the one involving the Whisky Rebellion came at a bad time. He was assailed as an extremist when he equated with treason the rebels' refusal to pay, and since his health was fragile at the time, the violent political row that ensued took a good deal out of him and undoubtedly increased his desire to leave public office, which he did a year later.

When in November, 1798, Alexander Hamilton wrote his wife, Elizabeth, about the "sweet project" which he declared in that playful couplet would defy guessing, he had been on the American mainland for twenty-six years. He had been married to Elizabeth for eighteen years. He and his wife then had six children whom they sought to protect from the contagions that struck New York during the late spring, summer, and early autumn months. In 1793 Hamilton himself had almost succumbed to yellow fever. He was never as vigorous physically after the attack, though through sheer drive and determination, he managed to do a prodigious amount of work as a lawyer and to emerge as a leader at the Bar of New York.

There are several references to "the fever" in Hamilton's correspondence, with no tangible clue to the precise ailment involved. For instance, his friend James McHenry, who finished Henry Knox's unexpired term as Washington's Secretary of War and continued in the same capacity under John Adams, wrote Hamilton: "I have been a second time on the point of gaining immortality. . . . My dear Hamilton, adieu. . . . Remember me . . . who thinks it unbecoming the dignity of man to leave his part merely because it does not please him. I am melancholy you perceive. This plaguy fever has torn me to pieces."

Sometimes the references are to "yellow fever," although such specific designations are few. Mainly they spoke of "the fever" or "the plague." There were sharp differences of opinion as to what brought on these maladies since diagnostic skills had not yet advanced importantly. However, on one point there was virtual agreement: that a family could minimize the risk of contracting "the fever" by moving to the country.

* * *

Hamilton's declaration, in announcing his "sweet project" to Elizabeth: "I rely that you will cooperate with me cheerfully," was not a routine statement. It was an acknowledgment that his wife would have her hands full with two widely separated establishments to look after, since the family would occupy the town house during the winter months. But the problems involved, chief of which was transportation, in no way diminished Elizabeth Hamilton's enthusiasm. She was eager to proceed with her husband's "scheme," as he also called it, even after he reminded her that his law practice would continue to require trips to what were then considered far-off places: Albany, Philadelphia, New Haven, etc.—journeys that would in all probability compel his absence at times when work on the country house was in progress. He would have liked to have been available in New York for any contingencies that might arise, thereby shielding Elizabeth, who had six children to look after and many household responsibilities, from further duties. In addition, the orphaned daughter of Colonel Autle, a Hamilton comrade-in-arms who was killed in the Revolutionary War, lived with the Hamiltons as a member of the family. She was educated and treated in all respects as their own daughter.

In a joint venture with John Barker Church, the husband of Mrs. Hamilton's eldest sister, Hamilton rented a country house in Harlem for occupancy by the two families during the summer and autumn of 1798. Although this cannot be fully documented, it seems that both families were seeking to determine how well they could adjust to life in a so-called outlying district.

Hamilton's half of the rental was $37.50. A diligent study of available sources has failed to turn up information as to the exact location but it was ". . . a country house in the neighbourhood of what was afterward his own estate."

The experimental rental was apparently a success for it was at the termination of the summer-autumn occupancy, after the family had returned to its downtown home, with its better heating facilities and accessibility to tutoring schools and visiting tutors, that Hamilton wrote Elizabeth the letter about his "sweet project."

It is quite possible that this temporary country home, in conjunction with their successive town houses at Liberty and Partition Streets, was the one the Hamiltons occupied from 1800 to 1802 while The Grange was being built.

2

Hamilton had achieved wide acceptance as a lawyer. Now that he was practicing again he was offered many cases, sometimes more than he could handle. Although he was overworked he found joy in the thought that the harder he worked as a lawyer the nearer to realization would be his dream of a soundly financed home in the country.

Some years earlier he had ignored the advice of his close friend, Dr. James McHenry, a physician whose services were in great demand: "Have we not both of us continued long enough in the service of the public? Should I not exercise my profession and should not you? . . . I find that to be dependent upon a father is irksome, because . . . it is in my power to be independent by my own endeavours. I see that the good things of this world are to be purchased with money and that the man who has money may be whatever he pleases. . . ."

Despite all this emphasis on personal gain, when President John Adams asked McHenry, a Washington appointee, to continue as Secretary of War, the doctor was delighted, even though his salary as a cabinet officer compared unfavorably with what he had previously earned as a physician. The jauntiness of his letters to Hamilton (written after he had recovered his health) would seem to indicate that his homily on the magic power of money was more an exercise in rhetoric than a real conviction.

Although Ralph Waldo Emerson had not yet been born, James McHenry was an Emersonian in spirit. He early practised some of the philosophic notions that Emerson was to enunciate many years later. McHenry was not capable of such Emersonian eloquence as:

"A foolish consistency is the hobgoblin of little minds, adored by little statesmen and philosophers and divines. With consistency a great soul has simply nothing to do. . . . Speak what you think today in words as hard as cannon-balls, and tomorrow speak what tomorrow thinks in hard words again, though it contradict everything you said today."

McHenry *was,* however, capable of requesting that Hamilton return to government service without even bothering to ask the cabinet-officer-turned-lawyer to forgive him for his inconsistency. The undeclared war with France was assuming dangerous proportions and key figures in the Adams Administration were devoting more and more thought to the need for the services of someone capable of organizing the government's resources for a possible all-out war with France. His reputation for patriotism and integrity, his known willingness to make sacrifices, the soundness of his fiscal policies, and his brilliant record as a statesman and administrator made it inevitable that Hamilton would be the man chosen for the job. After formally accepting, he sent McHenry an informal letter on January 7, 1799. Its main purpose was to confirm the understanding that while he would accept no new commissions from clients, he would continue handling the cases of present clients who were willing to take a chance on his ability to represent them adequately while discharging the heavy responsibilities of an exacting government post. Without this dispensation he would have had to scrap his plans for a country house. The two jobs—as co-ordinator of resources for the quasi-war, and as a practicing attorney—meant that Hamilton was destined to work more than ever. This is probably the reason for the many "indispositions," a generic term in those days for almost any kind of illness, he suffered during the period 1798–1800 when he returned to the service of his country.

In his personal letter to McHenry he said:

". . . I have discontinued my practice as attorney and solicitor, from which I have derived a considerable part of my professional profits; . . .

"The very circumstance of my having accepted a military appointment, from the moment it was known, withdrew from me a large portion of my professional business. This, it will be perceived, was a natural effect of the uncertainty of my being able in the progress of suits to render the services for which I might be engaged, at the customary previous expense to the parties.

"The result has been, that the emoluments of my profession have been diminished more than one half, and are still diminishing, and I remain in perfect uncertainty whether or when I am to derive from the scanty compensations of the office even a partial retribution for so serious a loss.

"Were I rich, I should be proud to be silent on such a subject. I should acquiesce without an observation as long as any one might think the minutest public interest required an accumulation of sacrifices on my part. But after having to so advanced a period of my life devoted all my prospects of fortune to the service of the country, and dependent, as I am, for the maintenance of a wife and six children on my professional exertions, now so seriously abridged, it is essential for me to forego the scruples of delicacy, and to ask of you to define my situation. . . ."

The phrase "were I rich" that opens the preceding paragraph is an ironic reminder that Hamilton declined financial aid from General Philip Schuyler, his wealthy father-in-law. From beginning to end, The Grange project was beset by financial difficulties; monetary assistance from General Schuyler would have made the country house a reality much sooner.

While Hamilton accepted Schuyler's generous gifts—beams for the building of The Grange, a team of horses, and an occasional quarter of beef—he persisted in his refusal to accept the proferred funds. He imposed the same restriction on his wife. To a few intimates who knew the situation, Hamilton seemed too strict in the pursuit of his point. Hamilton was Hamilton, however, and could not be moved from what he considered the correct course. The letters of Mrs. Hamilton disclosed that her husband preferred the role of giver. For instance, when his father and his brother James mentioned in their letters that they needed money, it was promptly forthcoming.

It was known to General Schuyler that Hamilton had undertaken his government assignment even though he had not been feeling well when the tender was made. On February 1, 1799, only three weeks after Hamilton had written McHenry, we find Schuyler writing his daughter as follows:

"My dear beloved Eliza: I am deeply affected to learn that my beloved Hamilton is much indisposed. Too great an application to business and too little bodily exercise have probably been the cause of his disorders, immersed as he is in business, and his mind constantly employed he will forget to take that exercise, and those precautions which are indispensable to his restoration. You must therefore, my Dear Child, order his horse every fair day, that he may ride out, and draw him as frequently from his closet as possible . . . try to prevail on him to quit the busy scene he is in, and to pay us a visit accompanied by you. . . ."

There are no records to show whether Elizabeth ever had a chance to implement her father's advice. The heavy demands of Hamilton's schedule—his responsibilities in connection with the undeclared war, and application to the problems of law clients whose fees would speed the materialization of The Grange—make it seem unlikely that Hamilton had any time during this strenuous period for the horseback riding that General Schuyler recommended.

There is ample evidence that Hamilton never lost sight of his country-home goal, that he never wavered in his determination to go through with the plan. In *The Intimate Life,* published fifty-eight years ago, we read, "After some search Hamilton found a tract of land to his liking which today is that roughly bounded by St. Nicholas and Tenth Avenues, and which extends from 141st to 145th Streets, but formerly was much larger in extent, the western limit being the Hudson River. The Albany or Bloomingdale Road which passed diagonally through it has, of course, now entirely disappeared, but undoubtedly divided the part upon which the house stood from the farm on the easterly side." Street designations have changed since that book was published. Today The Grange is situated at Convent Avenue near West 141st Street, where it was moved late in the 1890s from a site one-and-a-half blocks north. An infinitesimal amount of the original land remains. The frame building is so close to St. Luke's Episcopal Church to the south and an apartment building to the north that there is no room to walk on either side.

Hamilton's friend, General Ebenezer Stevens, then a prosperous merchant, had a country place bordering on the site Hamilton liked best of the properties he had had a chance to inspect, and on October 25, 1799, he wrote Stevens as follows:

"If the owner of the ground adjoining you will take Eight Hundred pounds (£800) for sixteen acres including a parcel of woodland, and lying on the water the whole breadth, you will oblige me by concluding the bargain with him, and I will pay the money as soon as a good title shall appear. If he will not sell a part at this rate, I request you to ascertain whether he will take Thirty pounds an acre for the whole tract and let me know.

"If I like it, after another view of the premises, I shall probably take the whole at this price. But I can only pay one half down, a quarter in six months and the remaining quarter in a twelve month. He shall be satisfied on the score of security if he desires.

Yrs with regard,
A. Hamilton."

It is appropriate that Hamilton chose to build his country home in Harlem. For it was in an engagement at Harlem Heights with the British in 1776, in the bleak early days of the Revolution, that he first distinguished himself as a soldier.

Because chroniclers of the Hamilton saga disagree on a number of points, it should not perhaps be surprising that one biographer does not believe Hamilton distinguished himself in the skirmish—most historians avoid calling it a battle—at Harlem Heights. The dissenting writer gives a picture of young Hamilton as an ineffective officer who "lost all his baggage and one of his cannon." He gives as his source a manuscript, now in the Library of Congress, called "Mulligan's Narrative." The author of the biography in which Mulligan is quoted warns the reader in a footnote in the back of the book that Mulligan's story "must be scrutinized with great caution." One wonders whether the cautionary word should not have been published up front.

Actually Hamilton discharged his military responsibilities at Harlem in a manner that brought him to General Washington's attention and led to his appointment as a member of Washington's staff. Hamilton was cited for his skill in drilling his command and his contribution to the fortification of Harlem Heights.

Writers who have projected the Hamilton story in histories and biographies have frequently found it necessary to resort to the deductive method of reasoning, as witness such phrases as "under the circumstances it seems tenable that . . . ," "one may assume that . . . ," "it is within the realm of possibility that. . . ."

Under the circumstances it seems tenable that Hamilton had a sentimental interest in Harlem which he would not have enjoyed if his actions there had been less than satisfactory. Harlem had given him his start; it had brought him to Washington's notice. All other things being equal, it was natural for him to give Harlem first consideration in planning a country home not too distant from his Wall Street law office and his town house.

In 1789, thirteen years after he had participated in the military action on Harlem Heights, when Federal Hall in New York City was the first Capitol of the United States of America, and Washington was serving his first term as President, Alexander and Elizabeth Hamilton on many occasions rode northward with President and Martha Washington in the Presidential carriage over

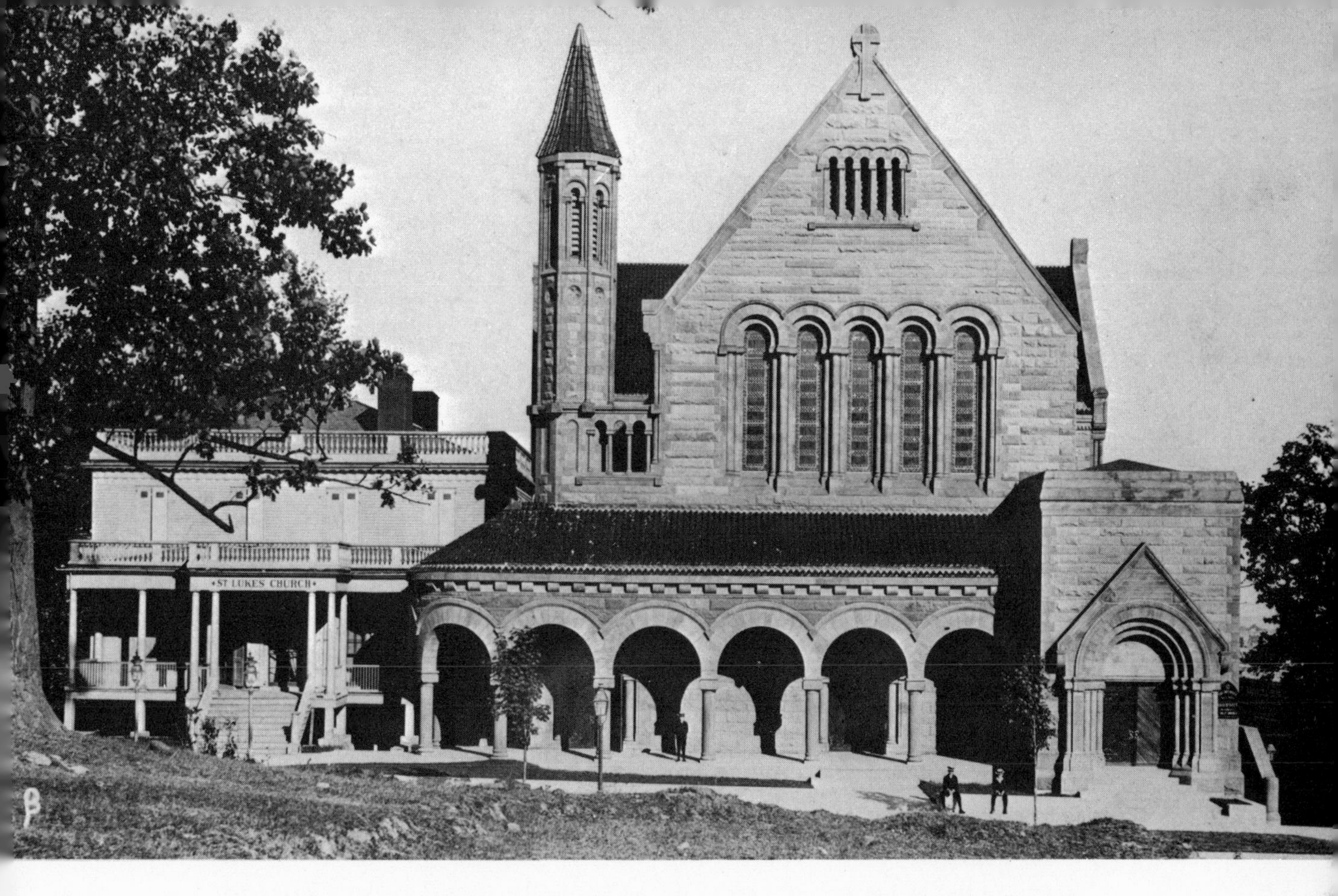

The Grange as it looked in the early 1890s, after the completion of St. Luke's Church. The sign over the front stairs indicates that The Grange was used at the time as an adjunct to the church. St. Luke's originally acquired The Grange solely for the land on which it stood, and there was talk of demolishing the house, which was in a woeful state of disrepair.

Isaac Tuttle (Rector Emeritus of St. Luke's) put up a battle to save The Grange and paid for necessary repairs out of his salary. A new roof alone cost Tuttle $1,500

the old Bloomingdale Road, passing through the inevitable Harlem before making the return trip to lower Manhattan. Harlem and Hamilton seemed inextricably intertwined.

3

Coming at a time when Hamilton was struggling with the problem of paying for the land on which he planned to build his country house, the lawsuit that became known as Le Guen *vs.* Gouverneur & Kemble was a godsend. It brought him enhanced prestige as a lawyer and a fee that was substantial for that time (though modest in terms of what Hamilton accomplished). It was the most important commercial case of his whole career. (From the national standpoint his most significant and far-reaching case was the People *vs.* Croswell, best known today to scholarly specialists in American jurisprudence for the compelling reason that, to a great extent, it established the present law of libel in the United States. Although this case did not figure as importantly in the Alexander Hamilton economy as the Le Guen *vs.* Gouverneur & Kemble lawsuit, it seems appropriate to mention that it also made its contribution to the economy of The Grange.)

In Le Guen *vs.* Gouverneur & Kemble, both sides were shipping merchants and both wanted Hamilton to represent them, a tribute to his renown as a lawyer. The issue was "the alleged misrepresentation and substitution of a cargo of indigo, cotton and other substances."

Hamilton's involvement in this lawsuit came as the near-war with France was ending. After Secretary of War McHenry agreed that his services were no longer needed by the government, it was possible for him to make his second exit from the service of his country and to devote his full time and attention to his law practice.

Le Guen *vs.* Gouverneur & Kemble, which Hamilton referred to as the Le Guen case, was tried in Albany, New York, and was widely reported in the press of the time. In the published allusions to court-room scenes there are references to Gouverneur Morris's "honeyed tones," "mellifluous voice," "compelling presence," a "delivery suggesting an accomplished actor declaiming lines in a play," etc., whereas the emphasis in the descriptions of Hamilton is on his crisp, businesslike approach to the case and his unfailing politeness—a word which emerged as *politesse*—in dealing with his adversary even when replying to scornfully phrased asseverations.

Here is a quotation from an account of the trial:

"This great case, which was ultimately decided in the Court of Errors, led to much subsequent litigation. Le Guen, a Frenchman, was represented by Hamilton, Burr, and others, and the defendants by Gouverneur Morris and associates. The counsel were permitted by the court to speak repeatedly out of the ordinary course, so great was the interest and desire to get at all the facts. Morris was most offensive to Hamilton in court, and there was an interchange of retorts between the two, and the 'commanding' figure, melodious voice, and authoritative manner of the former made a great impression." In his *Reminiscences* James A. Hamilton refers to this.

"Morris, during his argument and after speaking in praise of what Hamilton had said, used these words: 'Before I have done I am confident I shall make my learned friend cry out, Help me, Cassius' (pointing to Burr) 'or I sink.'

"When Hamilton's turn came to reply, he treated Morris with great courtesy, reviewed his arguments without mercy, exposing all their weakness, and then alluded to the boast of his friend in a strain of irony that turned the laughter of the court and audience against him."

Hamilton's clients, a group of merchants whose interests had been heavily damaged by a series of involved maneuvers, won spectacular redress. It was the biggest monetary award a plaintiff had been granted in a commercial suit up to that time, and now more than ever Hamilton was considered the foremost lawyer of the land.

In keeping with the custom of the times, after a verdict had been rendered in a major lawsuit, "There was a dinner given to the counsel, judges, and others, by Stephen Van Rensselaer of Albany, the patroon."

Hamilton had dressed for dinner at the house of his father-in-law, General Schuyler, who lived in Albany.

"When Hamilton arrived," the narrative continues, "Van Rensselaer met him at the door, and to put him on his guard, informed him that Morris was in a very bad humour.

"Hamilton went into the room, approached Morris most amiably, and said: 'My friend, you will rejoice, I hope, that by Cassius's help I meet you here with our friends at dinner.' "

This was Hamilton's way of acknowledging, in the presence of others, the effectiveness of Burr's assistance and Burr was pleased.

As has been stated, the Le Guen case was the most important *commercial* case of Hamilton's career. It might be added that from the standpoint of public relations, an expression that did not come into being until well over a century later, it was the case that would have made Hamilton a rich man had he lived long enough. Since it resulted in an ever mounting interest in his work, eventually he would have had to retain a large staff of associates to accommodate all the business he could have had. Some scholars doubt whether he ever would have established a large law office, because as a stickler for the personal touch, he would not have accepted cases which would have had to be handled by remote control.

The Le Guen case contributed more than *any* other of Hamilton's cases to his exchequer, and coming when it did, it made possible the purchase of the land on which the Hamilton Grange was to be built a few years later. The importance of the Le Guen case, however, may go beyond its contribution to The Grange project and its spectacular enhancement of Hamilton's reputation as a lawyer. The fact that in 1800 Hamilton was sufficiently friendly to Aaron Burr to invite him to join in the preparation of so momentous a lawsuit and the concomitant fact that Burr accepted the tender can be interpreted as meaning that the men were on reasonably good terms at the time. It may throw light on one of the causes of the feud between Hamilton and Burr on which conflicting views have been expressed by historians and biographers. The majority view is that the breach stemmed exclusively from developments of a political nature. Nathan Schachner, author of *Alexander Hamilton,* one of the most scholarly of Hamilton's biographers, pinpoints the break between the two men as having begun in 1791 when General Schuyler failed to get the nomination to succeed himself in the Senate.

". . . The dry routine of nomination and election exploded into sudden surprise," writes Schachner. "The name of Schuyler was rejected. And Aaron Burr, the young colonel of the Revolution, the brilliant lawyer with whom Hamilton was on fairly friendly terms, was chosen as the next Senator from New York. What had happened?

"Hamilton did not know—he attributed the disaster in fact to the secret and personal machinations of Aaron Burr, and reacted with such violence that a series of events was set in motion that ended ultimately in the tragedy of his own obliteration."

On May 1, 1800, approximately nine years later, Louis Le Guen wrote to Alexander Hamilton from New York. Here are the passages that are pertinent to this discussion:

"Still deeply moved by your generous proceedings, and full of gratitude, I find myself obliged to do what you yesterday forbade me to, confining myself to remitting you herewith the moderate sum of fifteen hundred dollars. Kindly accept it and at the same time the assurance that nobody in the world is more respectfully attached to you, or more disposed than I am to seize every opportunity to shew you all my gratitude. Therefore, dear General, be so kind as to make use of them, and also be well assured of the sincerity of my feelings, which will last as long as I live. . . .

"I also enclose a little account of what I have paid to Mr. Burr, including interest at seven per cent upon divers sums that I have advanced him amounting altogether to $4,636.66.

"I beg you to kindly settle this bill with him, so that he will be satisfied; he has promised to settle up with me tomorrow for the sum of 13,200 dollars that he owes me, fallen due the 15th of last month, the only business that keeps me here."

Louis Le Guen was unquestionably a devoted friend of Hamilton's but, quite unwittingly, he put Hamilton in an awkward position by giving him an assignment that involved dunning a fellow attorney. Burr, a proud man, must have regarded this obligation as a personal matter between himself and Le Guen and possibly resented being prodded in a matter involving a debt by the man who had congratulated him only a few days earlier for his contribution to the victory of Le Guen over Gouverneur & Kemble. This unfortunate situation may have been the beginning of a new Burr-Hamilton feud after they had patched things up after Burr's nomination to the Senate.

There will always be speculation as to what were the root causes of the ultimate antagonism between Hamilton and Burr. "Times change but human nature does not," commented a contemporary authority on politics when asked whether he thought the famous rift was political, "and it is hard to believe that their political differences alone led Hamilton and Burr to the dueling ground. I can cite examples of the most vicious vendettas during twentieth-century elections that subsequently saw the feudists bury the hatchet once the election was over. One can go back to the earliest days of our nation and cite parallel examples."

Inevitably some Shakespeare scholar will analyze the remark in which Gouverneur Morris, Hamilton's opposite in the Le Guen case, likened Burr to Cassius, one of the chief conspirators against Julius Caesar. The interpretation could be that Morris was alluding to Caesar's having sought the advice of

Cassius whom he mistakenly considered a friend. More tenuous points than this have been advanced by historians and biographers in an effort to get at the nub of the ultimate, irreparable Burr-Hamilton rift.

Thinking it might serve a useful purpose to have the opinion of a distinguished contemporary lawyer familiar with early American jurisprudence as well as the early history of the Republic, I consulted Arthur Moynihan, attorney for the Associated Press, and asked whether it were reasonable to suppose that Hamilton would have asked Burr to help him with the Le Guen case unless at that particular time the men were on good terms. Mr. Moynihan said it was inconceivable that Hamilton would invite Burr to join him unless the two lawyers could freely confide in each other. Developing his point, he stated that because of the explosive nature of many of the confidential documents involved, Hamilton could not have afforded to make Burr privy to the facts unless he could do so with a feeling of security. "The one thing that puzzles me," Mr. Moynihan concluded, "is why Hamilton chose Burr, who was not an experienced trial lawyer, for this assignment. The explanation probably is that Burr's prominence lent a certain amount of prestige."

It has been suggested that perhaps Le Guen requested Hamilton to accept Burr as co-counsel. Of course, anyone familiar with Hamilton's fierce independence need not be told that he would have rejected such a proposal if he had felt any uneasiness about Burr as an associate.

In addition to the dunning incident, Hamilton had written John Rutledge, who wielded great political influence, when he was alarmed by the possibility of Burr's becoming President. (Rutledge was a much-consulted "insider," having served with distinction as Governor of South Carolina and as Associate Justice of the Supreme Court.) In writing Rutledge, Hamilton stressed Burr's many large debts, including one amounting to $80,000. When the contents of Hamilton's letter to Rutledge became known, Burr, a hothead on the subject of his heavy indebtedness, was furious (since Hamilton was saying in effect that the President of the United States should not have a swarm of creditors). Hamilton's homily on Burr's debts, revealed shortly after he had served as Le Guen's bill collector, might have caused the final break with Burr.

Another passage from Hamilton's letter to Rutledge, in which Hamilton calls Burr "extortionate in his profession," may have been a reference to Burr's having charged more for his services as assistant counsel in the omnipresent

An elaborate French clock presented to Alexander Hamilton in 1800 by Louis Le Guen, who was represented by Hamilton in a famous lawsuit. It yielded the former Treasury Secretary's largest fee as a lawyer and helped make The Grange a reality

Le Guen case than Hamilton had as chief counsel. A study of Le Guen's records in the Allan Hamilton book could be interpreted as meaning that Burr received $1,400 more, although this is not a certainty.

These observations on the Le Guen case may seem to have taken us a long way from The Grange. But have they, really? The Le Guen fee helped create the Harlem country house, which, once built, became a place where the Hamiltons entertained the leading merchants of the time. The ramifications of this precedent-setting mercantile case, the most famous of the early 1800s, made good dinner conversation.

From the standpoint of The Grange, and the money needed to pay for the land and the building of the house, the most striking aspect of the Le Guen case is that although Hamilton had an acute financial problem he declined to accept the higher fee his client thought he merited. (Subsequently he found it necessary to borrow $5,000 from Le Guen to help lift his country-home project out of the realm of wishful thinking.) Hamilton had definite ideas about how much a lawyer should charge for his services and he could not be persuaded from these notions, regardless of how badly he needed money.

4

On August 2, 1800, Hamilton purchased from Jacob Schieffelin, designated in the Instrument of Conveyance as a "New York City Druggist," a parcel of land measuring "fifteen acres, one rood and ten perches in extent." It was in the neighborhood he had in mind when he wrote his letter to General Stevens. It will be recalled that Hamilton had stipulated a tract "lying on the water the whole," in other words, fronting on the Hudson River. When Schieffelin and his wife declined to part with the river-view acreage, he took the next best thing, land that ran steeply up a hill from what is now St. Nicholas Avenue, and extended northward from 141st to 145th Streets. With nothing to obstruct his view, from his hilly eminence Hamilton could look westward and take in the magnificent sweep of the Hudson River and the Palisades of the New Jersey shore.

Many New Yorkers in those days were not sure whether the area that embraced the site of the future Grange was physically a part of New York City itself. It took in a number of farms and was considered by many an "outlying district," a suburb of the city, although not so designated. An old newspaper clipping describes it as being "in the outskirts." And, as mentioned earlier, some called it Manhattanville.

In view of the foregoing it is interesting to note that the Instrument of Conveyance describes the Hamilton land as being "at Haerlem in the Seventh Ward of the City of New York."

The *Magazine of American History,* in its issue of January, 1889, reported that this Instrument of Conveyance had not been recorded until 1827. In a letter written April 22, 1929, which is in the files of the American Scenic and Historic Preservation Society, the president of which is the present-day Alexander Hamilton (a direct lineal descendant of the first Secretary of the Treasury), Mrs. E. A. Clarke, Meadow Lawn, Seabright, New Jersey, stated:

". . . My grandfather, Mr. Greene Ward, at one time owned the Grange but I do not know how this deed of sale came into his possession. . . . I, or one of my brothers, will be glad to present the original bill of sale from 'Jacob Schieffelin and Hannah, his wife,' to Alexander Hamilton." She added that the presentation of this bill of sale would be made when the plan for the restoration of The Grange was consummated.

Despite his frequent absences from New York to accommodate out-of-town clients, Hamilton was the driving force behind the building of The Grange throughout its construction. Before the house had even been designed he visited his newly acquired acreage to study it and consider the various possibilities for the location of the house. Whenever possible, usually on weekends, he would board the New York to Albany stagecoach, which started from the tip of lower Manhattan, made several downtown stops, and let him off at a point near his property. When Hamilton's schedule did not permit his taking the coach, or when all the seats were booked, he used his own carriage.

Later, after The Grange had been completed, the Albany stagecoach would let Hamilton off at his gate. Sometimes he also used the stagecoach to get to his office, but more frequently he relied on his own carriage.

The Grange was designed by John McComb, Jr., who incorporated in his plans the best of the suggestions he received from Hamilton and his father-in-law, General Philip Schuyler, who might be listed as assistant architects. McComb was a combination of open-mindedness and candor. He welcomed suggestions but did not hesitate to reject those he considered unpractical. The best-known public building that he designed is New York's City Hall; so far as is known, The Grange—or what remains of it—is the only example left of his work in the field of private dwellings.

On Monday, August 25, 1800, General Schuyler wrote Hamilton:

"My Dear Sir: Your favour of the 13th instant with the plan of your intended house was delivered me on Thursday last, that of the 18th by the mail I received yesterday. I have delivered Mr. Putnam the builder, the plan, and a paper of which you have a copy on the other side, and expect his answer tomorrow.

"If the house is boarded on the outside, and then clap boards put on, and filled in the inside with brick, I am persuaded no water will pass to the brick. If the clap boards are well painted, and filling in with brick will be little if any more expensive than lath and plaister, the former will prevent the nuisance occasioned by rats and mice, to which you will be eternally exposed if lath and plaister is made use of instead of brick.

"The partitions between the apartments in the interior of the house, if made of joice and then lathed and plaistered also have vacancies as receptacles for rats and mice. It is a little but not much more expensive to have the partitions of plank of 2 or 2 1/2 inches thick set vertically from floor to ceiling and joined together, but not planed, on these planks the lathes and plaister are to be put, and thus a solid partition is formed. In the bill of scantling which you have sent me I do not find any timbers for the gutters. . . .

"Should Mr. Putnam refuse to contract unless for the whole house in all its parts, except the masonry, I will receive his proposals on a statement which I shall make and transmit it to you without delay, or should he be extravagant in his demand, I shall . . . go up and contract for the timber and purchase the boards and planks, and if possible I will cause the boards and planks to be put into water for two months and then piled up with decks between them that they may be seasoned before they are worked up. . . .

"It will save very considerable expense if the clap boards and boards for the floors were sawed to the proper breadth and thickness at the sawmills, therefore I wish you to send me how many of each . . . will be wanted, their breadth and thickness. I rejoice, my dear son, that my Philip has acquitted himself so well, and hope that his future progress may correspond with your and my wishes.

"All here unite in love to you, my Eliza and the children. I am my dear Sir

Ever most affectionately yours,
Ph. Schuyler

"To Honble M. Gen. Hamilton."

The Philip referred to in General Schuyler's letter was Alexander Hamilton's eldest son, a student at Columbia College. He was killed less than two years later, before he was twenty, in a duel with a young lawyer named George I. Eacker. Philip and Eacker, a partisan of Aaron Burr, had quarreled over politics and such was the code of the times that they challenged each other on a "field of honor" in Weehawken, New Jersey. The death of Philip had a shattering effect on Alexander and Elizabeth Hamilton. They were heartbroken, and to commemorate the memory of their slain son, their youngest child, born in 1802, was also named Philip. To add to the misfortunes of the Hamiltons, so great was the impact of Philip's death on his eldest sister, Angelica, that in time she became deranged. Many doctors were called in in an effort to save her but Angelica did not respond. She remained insane until her death at the age of seventy-three.

Progress on the building of The Grange was proceeding at a satisfactory rate and the structure was well on the way to completion when Philip was killed. A study of available data, mainly letters, would seem to indicate a lag between Philip's death and the completion of the project, probably due to the protracted shock suffered by the grief-stricken parents.

Since McComb was one of the great architects of his time, considerable interest has been displayed in his work over the years and his method of operation. It is good to be able to publish a memorandum in which he sets forth some of the more basic aspects of the building of The Grange. In the early nineteenth century such documents were sometimes called "financial stipulations." Today they are known simply as estimates.

Under the title, "Proposal for finishing General Hamilton's Country House," appears this verbal blue-print:

"To build two stacks of chimneys to contain eight fire-places, exclusive of those in the Cellar Story.

"To fill in with brick all the outside walls of the 1st and 2nd stories, also all the interior walls that Separate the two Octagon Rooms—and the two rooms over them—from the Hall and other Rooms in both Stories.

"To lath and plaster the side walls of 1st and 2nd stories with two coats & set in white.

"To plaster the interior walls which separate the Octagon Rooms in both Stories, to be finished white, or as General Hamilton may choose.

"To lath and plaster all the other partitions in both Stories.

"To lath and plaster the Ceiling of the Cellar Story throughout.

"To plaster the Side walls of Kitchen, Drawing Room, Hall & passage, & to point & whitewash the Stone & brick walls of the other part of Cellar Story. To point the outside walls of Cellar Story and to fill in under the Sills.

"To lay both Kitchen hearths with brick placed edge ways.

"To put a Strong Iron back in the Kitchen fire-place five feet long by 2 1/2 9″ high.

"To put another Iron back in the Drawing Room 3′–6″ by 2′–9″.

"To place two Iron Cranes in the Kitchen fire-place—& an Iron door for the oven mouth.

"The Rooms, Hall, and Passage of the first story to have neat Stocco Cornices—Those of Octagon Rooms of Best Kind (but not inriched).

"To put up the two setts of Italian Marble in the Octagon Rooms, such as General Hamilton may choose—and Six setts of Stone Chimney pieces for the other Rooms.

"The Four fire-places in the Octagon rooms & the two rooms over them, to have Iron Backs and jambs, and four fire-places to have backs only.

"To lay the foundations for eight piers for the Piazza.

"Mr. McComb to find at his own expense all the Material requisite to the afore described work and execute it in a good & workmenlike manner for one thousand Eight Hundred & Seventy five Dollars.

"General Hamilton to have all the Materials carted and to have all the Carpenters' work done at his expense—

"General Hamilton is to find the workmen their board or to allow ____ shillings per day for each days work in lieu thereof.

"New York 22nd June 1801.

John McComb Jun."

Then, seemingly as afterthoughts, the following brief paragraphs were appended:

"To build the Stew holes and a wall for the sink.

"The whole to be completed by ________?"

None of the available documents tells us how the two blank spaces were filled in. This might have been arranged in an exchange of letters.

The contract to build the house went to Ezra Weeks, who superseded a builder named Putnam, the man originally considered. Putnam is mentioned in General Schuyler's letter to Hamilton, written August 25, 1800, in which Schuyler suggested the possibility that Putnam might prove "extravagant in his demand."

Hamilton did not worry any more than the average person building a house; he was content to take McComb's advice. McComb in turn permitted Hamilton those modifications that he thought practical. The only aspect that was a source of deep anxiety to Hamilton involved the chimneys. He considered a badly constructed one a fire hazard; he had also been in homes where the chimneys, while reasonably safe, smoked too much and made the occupants uncomfortable.

McComb shared Hamilton's concern about a "proper chimney." The leading authority on chimneys at the time was Benjamin Thompson of Woburn, Massachusetts, who had developed a reputation as a scientist on the subject. Allan Hamilton implies but does not specifically state that Thompson's recommendations on chimneys were followed. Whether they actually conferred with him is not known. Thompson had been forced to flee the country. The exact year he left is not known. His conservatism had invited suspicion, although the man was really a patriot. When his detractors realized they had wronged him he was permitted to re-enter the United States.

McComb and Hamilton "finally settled the matter, and the comfort of the inmates of the house was assured by the adoption of a proper chimney."

Benjamin Thompson spent his exile in Bavaria, where he rendered distinguished service as a scientist. When he returned to his native land he had an odd title the Germans had bestowed on him, the Count of Rumford, and in the early 1800s many an American home had a "Rumford Chimney." The most exhaustive research fails to disclose whether The Grange had Rumford-designed chimneys or whether McComb and Hamilton settled for following the Rumford principles.

5

In 1798 when Hamilton first told his wife about The Grange he undoubtedly planned to do more personal supervision of the project than events subsequently permitted. He probably attached no significance to the fact that he had found it necessary to hint at his plan in a letter, then await a respite from law-practice traveling to disclose the details of his "sweet project."

In a sense he was a victim of his own genius for efficiency. He had done so good a job of organizing his Wall Street law office that he was free to accept lucrative out-of-town commissions. Not much study of the record is required for one to realize that, by odd circumstance, a big percentage of his most important cases required what in those days amounted to considerable travel, or "journeying," as Hamilton sometimes called it. As far as The Grange was concerned, this relegated him to the role of supervisor-by-correspondence. During the period of approximately two years that it took to complete The Grange there was a constant flow of letters from Hamilton to his wife in which he gave instructions, made inquiries, and registered his point of view on all phases of the operation as clearly as a busy journeyman lawyer could.

Usually Hamilton traveled to his various destinations by stagecoach. Occasionally he used his own carriage, drawn by "Riddle," his favorite horse. On one such trip he wrote to Elizabeth:

". . . Somehow 'Riddle' sprained the ankle of one of his hind legs, which very much retarded my progress today. By care and indulgence, he is much better this evening.

"I have travelled comfortably and my health is better. Wife, child and hobby are the only things upon which I have permitted my thoughts to run. As often as I write, you may expect to hear something of the latter. Don't lose any opportunity which may offer of ploughing up the new garden spot and let the waggon make a tour of the ground lately purchased to collect the dung upon it to be scattered over that spot.

"When it is too cold to go on with grubbing, our men may be employed in cutting and clearing away the underbrush in the Grove and the other woods; only let the centre of the principal wood in the line of the different rocks remain rough and wild.

"The Country people all agree that to fat fowls, it is essential to keep them well supplied with gravel. One, of whom I inquired, informed me that sea shore gravel, not too large, is particularly good. They also say the coops must be cleaned out every two or three days. After the Fowls have had a sufficient opportunity of drinking, the remaining water must be removed."

Another time he sat down at the traveling desk that had a permanent place in his baggage to pass along to Mrs. Hamilton some afterthoughts he had had about a job of gardening done by one of his workmen. It involved the location of certain trees. After much reflection he decided that they had not been placed where he thought they properly belonged. So he sent his wife the inevitable instructions:

". . . Dunphy planted the Tulip Trees in a row along the *outer* fence of the Garden . . . and was collecting some Hemlock Trees to place between them. I desired him to place them in a row along the *inner* fence,—I mean the side nearest the house.

"But having attended to them in my route, I shall be glad, if White Pines are not conveniently to be had, that besides those along the inner fence there may be one Hemlock between every two of the Tulip Trees along the outer fence."

The harder one tries to visualize Alexander Hamilton as an itinerant attorney the more the picture amazes one. Here is a man seated in a stagecoach, or in his own carriage, who was once quoted in the *Daily Advertiser* to the effect that when he boarded a stage that would take him to the scene of a major trial he was not sure what occupied the greater amount of space in his baggage: the clothes or the legal documents and related memoranda. This reference to the voluminous records he frequently carried with him is ample proof that on these trips he usually had plenty on his mind.

However, The Grange was never completely excluded. On one of these journeys we find him ruminating in a Peekskill inn about the habitual dampness of the soil on which his orchard stood. He takes time out from his meditations on what he would say in court—he believed in previewing his own presentation and seeing if he could puncture it—to write Elizabeth one day about "those trees." His concern about them had temporarily succeeded in making him forget his client, and he seats himself at his portable desk, set on a table in his lodgings, and sends her a letter dated only October 16:

"I have just arrived here and shall stay till tomorrow.

"It has always appeared to me that the ground on which our Orchard Stands is much too moist. To cure this a ditch around it would be useful, perhaps with a sunken fence as a guard. . . .

"If you can obtain one or two more labourers, it may be adviseable to cut a ditch round the Orchard three feet deep by three feet wide at the bottom. The clay that comes out of the Ditch will be useful to give firmness to our road and may be used for this purpose."

Although he ends this letter by saying, "I confide this merely as a suggestion," there are indications that he had a way of following up his "suggestions" and insisting that they be carried out when he felt strongly about them.

Occasionally Mrs. Hamilton joined her husband when he was not too far away from the City of New York in pursuit of his profession. As much as he missed her, he discouraged such meetings when they involved a long journey. For instance, in a letter headed "On the Road to Albany," we find him writing her:

"The roads are too bad for you to venture in your carriage, if you can possibly avoid it.

"Don't forget to visit The Grange. From what I saw there, it is very important the drains should be better regulated. . . ."

This letter was written not long before his eldest son was killed in the duel with Eacker and we find in it a saddening reminder that Hamilton thought the young man capable of assuming responsibility: "Leave, in particular charge of Philip, what you cannot yourself accomplish."

That Mrs. Hamilton was a woman of spirit is evidenced by her willingness to undertake, by herself, the three-day journey to Albany where her husband was scheduled to try an important case. An injury to her horse—or damage to a carriage wheel, a common occurrence on those primitive roads—would have left her stranded and dependent on help from a passing stage or some friendly private conveyance. But she was eager to see her husband, as well as to visit her parents in their Albany home; and if Hamilton had not been so realistic about the hazards, she would have made the trip, especially as she was concerned at the time about her father's health.

The chances are that if Mrs. Hamilton had joined her husband at his destination, he would have, after inquiring about the children, given her detailed instructions about the drains at The Grange, which he thought should be "better regulated," supplemented perhaps by a drawing or diagram. Unfortunately only a few of his sketches have survived. They can best be described as hastily done and unpolished, but explicit.

Hamilton, preoccupied with the vast amount of work entailed in his lucrative out-of-town law practice, probably did not realize that his own letters were contributing factors to his wife's eagerness to join him, wherever he happened to be. Here is an example, written from Poughkeepsie on February 20, 1801, the only one of the few written during that period in which he does not mention The Grange:

"I am in much better health than spirits. In other words, I am more and more homesick. This, added to some other circumstances that do not give me pleasure at the present moment, makes me rather heavy-hearted. But we must make the best of those ills that cannot be avoided.

"The occupation I shall have at Albany will divert my mind from painful reflections; and a speedy return to my dear family will bring me a cure.

"Write me often, and receive every wish that is due the best of women.

"Kiss the children for me. Adieu."

One can only guess at what Hamilton meant by "some other circumstances that do not give me pleasure." For one thing, it took him a long time to recover from President Adams' sharp repudiation of his warlike stance *vis-à-vis* France. Still another factor could have been the financial difficulties that necessitated his postponing the purchase of the second parcel of land from the Bradhursts. It was only a fraction of an acre smaller than the original expensive acquisition of the first fifteen acres from the Schieffelins and represented a substantial outlay. Without this additional land The Grange would not have the spacious grounds that Hamilton had visualized from the beginning.

* * *

There was a farmhouse on the land the Hamiltons bought from the Schieffelins which supposedly stood on the north corner of the property. Under the supervision of Architect McComb this dwelling was repaired, and the Hamiltons used it as a country home until The Grange was ready for occupancy. McComb's bill was $70.90. A study of the itemization reveals that extensive repairs could be made in 1800 for this sum.

The Hamilton children, during the first year of their temporary occupancy of the "north cottage," were Philip, 18; Angelica, 16; James Alexander, 12; John Church, 8; William Stephen, 3; Eliza, 1. Another son was born in 1802. Also considered a member of the family was Colonel Autle's daughter.

With the exception of Philip, there is no record that Hamilton spent much time disciplining his children. Whether special attention was given to Philip because, as one source believes, the young man was a "sad rake," or whether, as another source believes, Hamilton was convinced of his son's "future greatness" and sought to correct a tendency toward wildness, Hamilton decided that a strict regimen was indicated and prepared these regulations for his son's guidance:

"Rules for Mr. Philip Hamilton:

"From the first of April to the first of October he is to rise not later than six o'clock; the rest of the year not later than seven. If earlier, he will deserve commendation. Ten will be his hour of going to bed throughout the year.

"From the time he is dressed in the morning till nine o'clock (the time for breakfast excepted), he is to read law. At nine he goes to the office, and continues there till dinner-time. He will be occupied partly in writing and partly in reading law.

"After dinner he reads law at home till five o'clock. From this time till seven he disposes of his time as he pleases. From seven to ten he reads and studies whatever he pleases.

"From twelve on Saturday he is at liberty to amuse himself.

"On Sunday he will attend the morning church. The rest of the day may be applied to innocent recreations.

"He must not depart from any of these rules without my permission."

These rules were posted in Philip's room in the temporary cottage while The Grange was being built and in his room in the Hamilton home on Partition Street.

How much time the Hamiltons spent in The Grange while it was nearing completion is not known. There is ample evidence that the family, or part of it, occupied some of the rooms while the builder finished the construction job.

It is hard to determine whether Philip left for his duel with Eacker from Partition Street or from Harlem. When Philip was irrevocably committed to fight Eacker, he sought—and received—his father's advice. Apparently he felt free to do this. After all, there was no reference to dueling in the "Rules for Mr. Philip Hamilton." In a period notable for the common sense of most of the people, some of the leading figures of the time had out-of-the-ordinary notions on "defending one's honor."

6

As Secretary of the Treasury, Hamilton was known for his insistence on fastidious records of the minutest items of cost. It is therefore not surprising that there are records today showing what it cost to build The Grange, down to the last penny. For instance, we know that one Thomas Costigan, a "man-of-all-work," who rendered many services, beginning with the excavation and "doing all manner of work," performed services for three and one-half years and received a total of $424.50. Since the original parcel of land—to which two tracts were subsequently added—was not purchased from the Schieffelins until August, 1800, and since the main house of The Grange was completed two years later, undoubtedly Costigan was held over to work on the outbuildings. Construction or remodeling of a barn, a hen house, an ice house, a root house, and a shed was not completed until some time after the principal house was built.

Another workman, Thomas Dunnevan, according to an entry in the Hamilton expense book, was paid $152.18, "from the 8th of March, 1802, to the 4th of August, 1803, when the poor worthy fellow was drowned. Sixteen months and 27 days at 9d."

In addition to Costigan and Dunnevan, workmen identified as "Nash, Taylor, Nutter, Harris, Jennings, Malcolm and Tuff" were employed in the building of The Grange and received a total of $985.50. Their labors ceased in 1802.

It cost Hamilton $17,972.06 to build The Grange. It would serve no purpose to offer too detailed a breakdown of this figure. Wages were included in a "miscellaneous expenses" category, which also included such items as "pipes, cedar posts, house paint, blacksmith, carpentry." The total for this subdivision came to $2,152.01. The rest of the overall figure is made up as follows: "Schieffelen, for the ground, $4,000.00; Ezra Weeks, contractor, $9,324.85; John McComb, Jr., architect-contractor, $2,495.20."

One of the items on McComb's bill that catches the eye is a charge of $38.37 which represented "interest for delinquent payments under contract." Another is for $581.83 for "extras under the contract."

Apparently McComb made no special charge for drawing plans for the house. Presumably this was included in his basic estimate of $1,875.00.

The figure given as the overall cost of The Grange does not include the two parcels of contiguous land that Hamilton subsequently added, one a three-acre strip, the other a little over fourteen acres. Both were purchased from Samuel and Mary Bradhurst. The two parcels totaled seventeen acres, two roods and ten perches. Since the three-acre piece cost $750, a reasonably safe guess is that the larger parcel cost a little over $3,500. Adding this to the cost of The Grange with only the original Schieffelin acreage included, we get a total outlay for the buildings and over thirty-two acres of land of a little over $22,220.

Hamilton wrote to his old comrade-in-arms General Charles Cotesworth Pinckney, of South Carolina, from The Grange a few months after the project had become a reality:

"My Dear Sir: A garden, you know, is a very usual refuge for a disappointed politician. Accordingly I have purchased a few acres about nine miles from town, have built a house, and am cultivating a garden.

"The melons in your country are very fine. Will you have the goodness to send me some seed, both of the water and musk melons? My daughter (Angelica) adds another request, which is for three or four of your paroquets. She is very fond of birds.

"If there be anything in this quarter, the sending of which can give you pleasure, you have only to name them. As farmers, a new source of sympathy has arisen between us, and I am pleased with everything in which our likings and tastes can be approximated.

"Amidst the triumphant reign of democracy, do you retain sufficient interest in public affairs to feel any curiosity about what is going on? In my opinion, the follies and vices of the administration have as yet made no material impression as to their disadvantages. . . .

"Adieu, my dear Sir

Ever Yours,
Alexander Hamilton"

In designating himself a gardener and a farmer Hamilton was indulging in wishful thinking. His rapidly growing law practice, which involved still more and more travel, made it difficult for him to visit The Grange with any degree of regularity. Once he had thought of farming as a secondary career, a business from which he would derive both pleasure and profit. However, he was a realist and as more and more clients brought their problems to his office and minimized the amount of time he could spend in his country home, he began referring to The Grange in letters to his wife as a "hobby."

In describing himself as a disappointed politician, Hamilton may have had several ideas in mind. For instance, despite his stormy career in government service, he loved public office and would have enjoyed the opportunity of continuing to serve had he been a man of means as were so many of the familiar political figures of the time. Perhaps the word "despite" in the preceding sentence should be modified. Hamilton seemed to thrive on excitement; and it is quite possible that he found it stimulating to be in the thick of political combat.

So great was Hamilton's ability that the demand for his services transcended the common knowledge that he was hard to handle. In public life he did not hesitate to quarrel with his political sponsors, even political intimates, if he thought an important principle was involved. In piecing together his political credo, one finds that it has a uniformity, and that when he dissented it was not for dissent's sake.

Even had Hamilton had the time, it is hard to imagine him pacing the garden of The Grange and brooding over his political disappointments. He was of too philosophic a turn for that. It was a philosophy that demanded activity, contact with people and their problems, and he found ample opportunity for this in the practice of law.

There is no doubt that in the garden of his mind Hamilton did a lot of mental pacing, in the course of which he thought a great deal about some of his setbacks in public life. He had suffered so many political disappointments that it would be strange if he did not try to seek out the reasons for them. He had too analytical a mind not to do so.

When Secretary of War McHenry invited Hamilton, at the request of President John Adams, to return to government service only three years after he had resigned from Washington's cabinet, Hamilton must have been astounded. He had tried to prevent Adams' election. In fact, the failure of his efforts to block the Adams candidacy was one of Hamilton's early disappointments. Adams had the stature to believe that the country was entitled to Hamilton's services whether the former Secretary of the Treasury was an Adams partisan or not. Hamilton showed stature too because, at a personal sacrifice, he accepted an appointment from a man who had never gone out of his way to be friendly to him.

Another disappointment for Hamilton was that President Adams, while he recognized the merits of what Hamilton had done as an organizer and coordinator in putting the country on a war footing, was alarmed by Hamilton's militancy. He did not want war any more than Adams did but he believed in "talking tough" to France. In fact, in an erratic moment he wrote a pamphlet criticizing President Adams' efforts to settle the issue peacefully, a pamphlet Hamilton's friends tried unsuccessfully to recall. This contentious manifesto, which was not well received by the public, may have cost Hamilton consideration for the Presidency. It is not known whether or not he had Presidential ambitions. Leading Federalists thought he had the stature.

The new nation was repelled by the thought of a militancy that might lead to warfare at a time when it was struggling to get on its feet. Hamilton had made a gross miscalculation and there are no signs that any tears were shed when for the second time he returned to private life. This seems to have been his major disappointment; in all probability it was what he had principally in mind when he wrote General Pinckney the letter from The Grange which contains that most widely quoted of Hamiltonisms: "A garden, you know, is a very usual refuge of a disappointed politician."

However, Hamilton had made serious miscalculations before and had survived them; and it is hard to believe that he would not have tried to stage a political comeback if he could have afforded it. Throughout his career he was a fighter. His character was not to fade out under fire without subsequently attempting to make some official return to politics, if only to give himself the opportunity to retire later without the embarrassment of repudiation.

One of his friends described Hamilton as having "nine political lives," an accurate summation. One of these lives was snuffed out when as a delegate to the Constitutional Convention he was outvoted by the Antifederalists in his attempt to impose a strong central government to which the states should be completely subordinated. He was unhappy about this reversal but it did not discourage him. He more than compensated for the resultant temporary loss of prestige by his great contribution to the ratification of the Constitution. He was flexible enough to accept the majority view of what that instrument should stipulate, and it is generally conceded that the combined leadership of Hamilton and Madison was largely instrumental in bringing about its adoption.

There are so many ironies in Hamilton's life that one could write a book about those alone. One that comes to mind is that his political philosophy of the subordination of states rights to a strong central government, which so many considered heresy in his own lifetime, is close to the beliefs of Franklin D. Roosevelt and Lyndon Johnson and, generally speaking, one of the basic tenets of today's liberals; and to their followers it would seem that time has finally caught up with Alexander Hamilton.

If the ghost of Hamilton walks The Grange and it learns that its corporeal antecedent had been close to two twentieth-century Presidents in his thinking, it will undoubtedly want more information. For Hamilton never accepted a compliment without being satisfied with the source; therefore one can imagine some such reply as, "Tell me more about Roosevelt and Johnson."

It was typical of Hamilton to try to draw out his friends in political matters. This would explain the provocative nature of the last two sentences of his letter to Pinckney. The General, however, avoided being drawn into political discussion. In his reply he confined himself to such matters as are to be found in these excerpts:

"My dear Sir: I wrote you a few lines yesterday and sent you some watermelon seeds and musk-melon seeds by the brig *Charleston Packet* which sails this morning. I formerly sent some to Mrs. Washington, at Mount Vernon, but she told me they did not answer so well as some she got in the neighbourhood; perhaps had she planted the seeds from the melons which were produced from the Carolina seed the subsequent year, they would have adapted themselves to the climate and produced good fruit.

"It is by this means we obtained our fine cotton, which has been of such advantage to our state. The first year it produced but three or four pods; by planting the seed of these pods the second year, they produced thirty; and by following the same method, the third year they were thoroughly naturalized, and bore from one hundred and fifty to two hundred pods.

"I will also send you by the brig *Industry* a few seeds of the salvia cocinea, or scarlet sage, which I believe you have not with you, and of the . . . coral shrub; also a few seeds of the Indian creeper, and some of a beautiful purple convolvulus.

"I will endeavor to obtain some paroquets for Miss Hamilton. I have not seen any for some years; ours are the large kind, by no means equal in beauty to the small African species."

General Pinckney addressed himself exclusively to Gardener Hamilton. Like many another friend of Hamilton's, Pinckney knew that if he agreed or disagreed on the "follies and vices of the administration," his former comrade-in-arms would draw him out on different aspects of his views. Hamilton had an insatiable curiosity about people's political opinions, and since he was incurably controversial, there were those who withheld their beliefs. It was easier to send seeds and hope that Hamilton would assume that the General had simply forgotten to add his political opinions to the packages addressed to The Grange and placed aboard the *Charleston Packet* and the *Industry.*

Hamilton prided himself on his ability as a businessman. Some of his clients retained him to investigate "business opportunities" that had been offered them and to give his opinion as to the merits of these propositions. He was a thorough investigator and the indications are that as a business consultant his reputation was as good as it was in the field of law.

Before circumstances compelled him to define The Grange as a hobby, Hamilton had notions of himself as a businessman-farmer who would oversee the management of his acres and their produce and show a profit. Of course, he became an absentee farmer, and the Hamilton papers, well documented as to various financial aspects of The Grange, yield only one item dealing with revenue from the sale of produce (it is quite possible that this figure represents one of the few transactions of its kind that took place). In 1802 either Hamilton or his wife made a sale of strawberries, cabbages, and asparagus. The proceeds totaled £7.10.2. As the pound was worth $2.50 at the time, the sum realized was about $18. A descendant, commenting on this, wrote in 1910, "The experience of the amateur farmer then seems to have differed but little from that of most of us to-day."

Hamilton's chief mentor in the fields of agriculture and horticulture was his friend Dr. David Hosack, a distinguished and fashionable physician of the time whose interest in botany was almost as great as his interest in medicine. He was a graduate botanist, having started his studies in this field abroad, and was unique in that he eventually had two major titles at Columbia College, Professor of Materia Medica and Professor of Botany.

Hosack also became the Hamilton family physician. Dr. McHenry had occasionally ministered to Hamilton but had never been the family doctor. Since his interest in politics had resulted in government service that took him out of circulation for long periods of time, he had advised Hamilton to find a doctor who might not be taking the pulse of an ailing Federal department when needed by his patients.

The Hamiltons frequently consulted Hosack about the planting they planned at The Grange. Hamilton's letters reflect enough familiarity with botanical and agricultural matters to suggest that if he had not been forced by business contingencies into the role of absentee master of The Grange he probably would have met with greater success as a grower of vegetables and other marketable produce.

7

When General Schuyler's daughter informed him that The Grange was fast nearing completion, she reminded him that he was now expected to let her know when he, her mother, and other members of the family would be ready to pay their first visit. The bond between the Hamiltons and the Schuylers could not have been closer. As families they were bound by ties of the deepest affection, a relationship further strengthened by political ties. As author of fifty-one of the eighty-five essays that comprise the *Federalist* papers, that remarkable exposition of the Constitution and its aims, Hamilton emerged as the chief proponent of Federalism, and Schuyler was a prominent member of the party. Dedicated to the same political philosophy, and suspicious of any other, the two men can readily be imagined discussing politics at The Grange and taking pot shots at new developments they considered Antifederalist. Both were frank, outspoken partisans.

The Federalist Party had administered the government from 1789 to 1801, and it began losing its influence, by odd coincidence, in 1802, the year The Grange was completed. This must have made for much animated conversation when the two Federalist stalwarts put their heads together and told each other how the country should be run.

On August 22, 1802, General Schuyler wrote his daughter:

"I am anxious to visit you and to participate in the pleasure of your country retreat which I am informed is fast reaching perfection. Embrace my dear Hamilton and the children. He and they participate with you in your mother's and my warmest affection. May health and happiness be the portion of all. God bless you my dearly beloved child.

"I am ever, most tenderly and affectionately, yours,

Ph. Schuyler."

Allan McLane Hamilton, a consistently good source on Hamilton's "hobby," wrote:

"Life at The Grange was undoubtedly a merry one, for within its hospitable walls were gathered many of those clever people with whom Hamilton had so much to do during his many years of busy, official life. Gouverneur Morris often came from Morrisania, while Rufus King drove over from Jamaica, in Long Island, to discuss politics or gossip with the former Secretary.

"The Schuylers, too, came frequently, and sent good things from the Albany homestead, and in many of the General's letters are references to prodigious gifts of vegetables and fruit, which were consigned to his daughter by way of the river sloops, while in the winter it was rare for a beef to be slaughtered without a quarter finding its way to The Grange.

"The Hamilton family was often invited to Albany, and alluring accounts of what awaited them were drawn by the devoted father-in-law. General Schuyler wrote from Wood Creek, where he was journeying . . . , 'We have excellent mutton here, and as fine and fat salmon as ever were dished and I believe as cheap as cod at the New York market. I gave half a dollar for a

Silver-plated two-bottle wine cooler used at Mount Vernon, similar to a four-bottle wine cooler presented by George Washington to the Alexander Hamiltons. *De Butts Collection. Photograph courtesy of The Mount Vernon Ladies' Association*

very fine one weighing a little more than nineteen pounds. They are taken four miles from here.' "

It is interesting to note in the foregoing that "Gouverneur Morris often came from Morrisania." And the Hamiltons were the guests of the Morrises when the itinerant lawyer could find a place for such visits in his crowded schedule.

This, incidentally, meant that the Morrises had a properly functioning fireplace (or fireplaces). One of Hamilton's rules was that he would not accept an invitation to visit a house in which the fireplace was known to smoke. He liked to talk and maintained that a comfortable conversation was impossible when every time the speaker opened his mouth, he drew in smoke and wound up coughing and wheezing instead of stating what could be done to save the country. It was one of the reasons why, to prevent smoky fireplaces at The Grange, he went to extra expense in having them built.

Despite their acrimonious exchanges when they were on opposite sides in the courtroom, Hamilton and Morris remained good friends, which establishes that, at least in this area, human nature has not changed. Countless examples could be cited of prominent present-day lawyers who fight bitterly in court, then fraternize with each other after judge or jury have rendered a verdict.

The Rufus King referred to in the same passage was a delegate from Massachusetts to the Constitutional Convention in Philadelphia. Before he met Hamilton he was a staunch advocate of the supremacy of the states, with the federal government playing a subordinate role. His approach was very much like that of today's rhapsodic exponents of states' rights who take the position that "Washington cannot do that to *us,*" *that* meaning anything they happen not to agree with.

Hamilton, a powerful persuader, brought King over to his own view that the future of the country depended upon a strong centralized government as opposed to a mere aggregate of semi-independent states.

Like many a man who was ahead of his time, Hamilton suffered defeat. To the founding fathers, and this is understandable, there was a suggestion of monarchic rule in a Presidency vested with too much power. It was too clear a reminder of the British ruler whose tyranny the Revolutionary Colonists had fought, the King of whom it has been written:

George the Third
Should never have occurred.

Even when it was clear that the proposed Constitutional provisions that would irrevocably subordinate the states to the Federal government were doomed to defeat, King voted with Hamilton; for he believed that Hamilton was right. This cemented their friendship, and when King later moved to Long Island the men kept in touch with each other.

The Hamilton-King political credo, which some of their followers tried to keep alive, was in strong disfavor during the period when The Grange was built—1800 to 1802—and the year after, and it is not unlikely that when the men met at King's home or The Grange they discussed the chances of some day awakening the country to the need for a strong Federal government.

Hamilton knew how to modify his views and must have realized that there was one word that stood in the way of winning more converts to his opinion that the states should be subordinate to the Federal government. It was the word *completely*. He wanted 100 percent Federal domination, and when, as Allan Hamilton says, "Rufus King drove over (to The Grange) to discuss politics," it is well within the realm of possibility that the men exchanged views on others' lingering dissatisfaction with Hamilton's so-called extremism: his recommendation that to make Federal power supreme the President be given the right to veto any law passed by a state legislature or Congress that he considered a negation of his policies. This played into the hands of the opposition, who again and again raised the cry that it gave the Chief Executive sovereign power.

Rufus King, a full-time pragmatist, and Hamilton, at least a part-time one, must have given this particular aspect of the subject a good workout and might well have decided on a modification of their views. While Hamilton had seemingly forsworn official politics and further government service, his interest in public affairs never diminished; and it is not assuming too much to think that he looked forward to the day when, The Grange paid for and his family provided for, he could re-enter public life. It is reflected in his writings, shortly before and during The Grange period, that, politically, he had left much work to be done.

Another visitor to The Grange was John Jay, who had written five of the *Federalist* papers. Jay, the first Chief Justice of the United States Supreme Court, and Hamilton, the first Secretary of the Treasury, must have found plenty to talk about. One of Hamilton's enthusiasms was Jay's nationalistic opinion in *Chisholm vs. Georgia* (which eventually led to the passing of the Eleventh Amendment).

One of Hamilton's best friends was Richard Peters, formerly a judge of the United States District Court, who became a successful farmer and recognized writer on agricultural topics. Shortly after Hamilton resigned as Secretary of the Treasury, and only a few weeks after he had returned to the practice of law, he received a letter from Judge Peters, who was known as a jester, or "droll fellow," in the parlance of the times. "I was afraid of your being too idle," wrote Peters, "and have on this account put a teazing employment upon you," and asked his friend "to proceed against one Wm. Coghlan." It was a difficult case involving a land dispute of twenty years' duration. Major points of the case had been dimmed by the fog of time but Hamilton, a resourceful lawyer-sleuth, put the facts together and won the case. Although Hamilton had been a successful lawyer before he entered Washington's Cabinet, some members of the business community, remembering only his political prominence, did not think of him as someone who could be retained to try a case. Therefore when Peters recommended him to the leading merchants, whose need for legal services seemed inexhaustible at the time, it proved most helpful.

Hamilton and the judge-turned-farmer swapped letters. In one of them Hamilton confided:

"... The greatest part of my little farm will be dedicated to Grass. The soil is a sandy loam, in which there is rather too large a dose of sand. Yet every thing has hitherto thriven well.

"What will be my best plan as to the raising of Grass and what kind ought I to prefer; and what season for sowing the seed?"

In this same letter Hamilton expressed a sentiment with which he had opened the famous letter to General Pinckney mentioned earlier. There was very little difference in the phrasing, it was mainly a re-arrangement of the same words. To Pinckney he had written: "A garden, you know, is a very usual refuge of a disappointed politician." In the letter to Peters he put it this way: "A disappointed politician you know is very apt to take refuge in a Garden."

". . . my secretary in the country." Mahogany desk made in New York City in 1802 or 1803 for The Grange's library. *Owned by the Hamilton family*

Judge Peters sent a lengthy reply on January 8, 1803:

". . . I am glad you have this little Syren to seduce you from public anxieties. But take care that the meretricious charm of this new Flame does not make too great Drafts in your Purse. . . . Make your little Farm your Plaything, but see that you have other Business, that you may afford to pay for the Rattle. . . . I should be very happy to give you Instructions, in one of the few subjects you do not know better than I do. . . .

". . . The great mistake of young Farmers and the Disgrace of slovenly old ones, is to be in too great a Hurry in laying their grounds for grass. The Pests of bad precedent farming choak all their crops.

"Spare no Expense to destroy Weeds by cutting them before ripe, & frequent deep ploughing, with covering Crops. Weeds are the Jacobins of Agriculture. If you do not destroy them, they will certainly ruin you. French ploughing is the surest Way to get rid of them. If I can find a little Essay I wrote many years ago on this subject, I will send it to you.

"You must make compost of all the Trash of your Farm, mixed with what little Dung you have and lime or Cystic shells. Have you any Pond or River Mud? This with ashes to give it stimulus is good for your Land.

"I sow my grass seeds at all seasons, as circumstances require. On My Wheat Fields in February—with oats or Barley in the Spring also then with Flax—With Buckwheat in July—With Turnips in August. Timothy succeeds best in the Autumn. I cannot tell which is the best seed for your ground—if wet, Timothy—if dry red clover mixed with Timothy or orchard grass according to the situation. The latter absorbs the superabundant Juices of the Clover; & while growing preserves the crop from lodging or laying down. Salt your clover while you are putting it into the Stack or Mow. A Bushel to 4 or 5 tons. I would cheerfully send you clover seed, but we have none better than your own. Sowing it thick or thin makes it fine or coarse. I generally sow 8 pounds . . . to the Acre & I find it fine enough. . . ."

The foregoing indicates that when Hamilton wrote Peters "the greatest part" of his farm would be "dedicated to Grass" it was the same as saying he planned to be a hay farmer. Peters so interpreted it; for in those days the production of "grass," or hay, was considered fundamental. You raised "grass" for your own horses and, hopefully, for the market. There is a statement elsewhere in Judge Peters' long letter that further supports the theory that Hamilton had decided on hay-raising as his major agricultural activity:

"If you dedicate your Farm to Grass, divide it into small Fields; say 5 or 6 Acres each. Let them be well cultivated with cleaning Crops, so as to destroy all noxious Weeds."

How Hamilton fared as a hay farmer is not known.

Architect McComb's "Proposal for Finishing General Hamilton's Country House" enables us to visualize certain features of the structure, but only an account of the completed building can give us a rounded feeling of what it once was like. For the best and simplest description available (written in

1854) we now turn to the following from *Homes of American Statesmen,* which is in the files of the American Scenic and Historic Preservation Society:

"The house is nearly square, of moderate size and well proportioned. The front is on the southern side; it is two stories in height, exclusive of the basement, and would have been at the time it was built a handsome and expensive one. The basement is used for culinary purposes, and the first story, which contains the parlors, is reached by a short flight of steps. You enter a commodious hall of a pentagonal form. On either side is a small apartment, of which the one on the right was the study, and contained the library of Hamilton. At the end of the hall are doors, one on the right and the other one on the left, which open into the parlors. These are of moderate size and connected by doors, opening which they are thrown into one large room. The one on the right as you enter the house is now, and probably was when Hamilton occupied it, used as a dining room. The other parlor is furnished for the drawing room. It is an octagon in form, of which three sides are occupied by doors, leading to the hall in front, the dining room, and to a hall in the rear. In two of the opposite sides are windows reaching to the floor, and opening

Louis XVI-style sofa, originally installed in the parlor at The Grange in 1803. *Owned by the Hamilton family*

Chairs in the Louis XVI style made in 1802 or 1803 for Alexander Hamilton and used in the parlor at The Grange. *Owned by the Hamilton family*

upon the lawn on the easterly side of the house. The three doors before mentioned are faced with mirrors, and being directly opposite the windows, they throw back the delightful landscape which appears through the latter with a pleasing effect.

"The story above is commodious, and divided into the usual apartments. On the north the prospect is interrupted by higher ground, and on the south by trees. On the west a view is caught of the beautiful shore of New Jersey, on the opposite side of the Hudson. From the eastern side, and especially from the balcony which extends in front of the windows of the drawing room, a magnificent prospect is presented. The elevation being some two hundred feet above the surrounding waters, a complete view of the lower lands and of the country in the distance is commanded. Harlem with its river, the East River and Long Island Sound now dotted with a thousand sails, the fertile county of Westchester, and Long Island stretching away to the horizon, with its lovely and diversified scenery, are all in full view."

It is interesting to note that the author of the foregoing says of the Hamilton country house that it "would have been *at the time it was built* a handsome . . . one." (The italics are the writer's.) Later in this same account such adjectives as "delightful," "beautiful," and "magnificent" establish a mood that makes one think of The Grange as a Federalist version of the breathtaking edifice reared by Kubla Khan in Coleridge's famous poem. But of course those superlatives are more an endorsement of the view and the surrounding countryside than of the house itself.

Probably the most reliable esthetic estimate of The Grange as a house, divorced from the overpowering beauty of its original setting, is that of Allan McLane Hamilton. He was not the typical descendant of a distinguished forebear. The son of the Alexander Hamiltons' last child, Philip (named for the Philip who was killed in the duel with Eacker), Allan Hamilton revered his famous ancestor but could be objective about him and his works. In his *Intimate Life* he wrote:

"The Grange . . . was never an architectural triumph, although it is a type of comfortable country house of the period."

Allan Hamilton (who was born in 1848 and died in 1919) was a cultured man. After devoting many years to a career as a successful physician he decided to indulge his love of travel. A man of taste, he picked up many an art treasure during the extensive journeying that involved fifty Atlantic crossings. His books and the many magazine articles he wrote reflect the cultivated traveler with an eye for beauty. It is not surprising that a man of such proclivities and this general background could look at a structure like The Grange and pronounce its outlines "conventional," or that he was unhappy about certain details—for instance, the two chimneys. Since they were set on the roof awkwardly enough to offend the eye, two false chimneys were erected in balancing positions on the aft section of the roof.

Because Allan Hamilton calls McComb a distinguished architect, one wonders if the chimneys represented the thinking of Alexander Hamilton, the persuasive assistant architect who occasionally made forceful suggestions during the building of The Grange, sometimes directly to McComb, sometimes through Mrs. Hamilton.

8

An arresting footnote to the Hamilton-Peters friendship is that it was Peters who in February, 1811, about six and a half years after Hamilton's death, found a copy of Washington's Farewell Address in Hamilton's handwriting among his friend's papers. Although Mrs. Hamilton was still using The Grange at the time, it is unlikely that the Farewell Address was found there; in February The Grange, which was hard to heat adequately, was usually closed. Hamilton's study at his Harlem retreat had been the repository for many of his important records and memorabilia. Presumably when these papers were turned over to Judge Peters by Mrs. Hamilton for his opinion as to what should be preserved they had probably been previously removed from the study.

Peters called his discovery to the attention of John Jay, who had been so close to Hamilton; he informed Jay that still another copy had been found in the possession of "a certain gentleman" in the same handwriting. Jay was disturbed by the news, replying that "this intelligence is unpleasant and unexpected." He added that it might be presumed from these facts "that General Hamilton was the real and the President only the reputed author." This he doubted, he stated, for the reason that Washington was "a character not blown up into transient splendour by his great and memorable deeds, but stands, and will forever stand, a glorious monument of human excellence. . . . It was impossible for the President, because of his very greatness and the excellence of all his virtues and his familiarity with all the public affairs, to be anything else than the author of the document. . . ." It is clearly implied that a president who sought help in the writing of a speech was less than virtuous or an example of "human excellence." How times have changed!

This is no place for a lengthy discussion of the controversy that ensued for years as a result of the Peters-Jay correspondence. As late as 1859 William Jay, son of John Jay, published his "Inquiry into the Formation of Washington's Farewell Address." Oliver, a respected historian of the early 1800s, went so far as to say, "In September, 1796, Washington issued his Farewell Address, one of the most famous documents in American history, and this . . . was from Hamilton's pen." Binney, another contemporary authority on United States history of that period, stated as emphatically that Washington was undoubtedly "the original designer" of the Farewell Address: "The fundamental thought and principles were his, but he was not the composer or writer of the paper."

So many writers kept the subject alive that on August 7, 1840, at the urging of friends, Elizabeth Hamilton—who was eighty-two years old at the time—issued a lengthy statement on the subject. These passages are taken from it:

". . . A short time previous to General Washington's retiring from the Presidency in . . . 1796 General Hamilton suggested to him the idea of delivering a farewell address to the people on his withdrawal from public life, with which idea General Washington was well pleased, and in his answer to General Hamilton's suggestion gave him the heads of the subjects on which he would wish to remark, with a request that Mr. Hamilton would prepare an address for him; Mr. Hamilton did so, and the address was written. . . . He was in the habit of calling me to sit with him, that he might read to me as he wrote, in order, as he said, to discover how it sounded upon the ear, and making the remark, 'My dear Eliza, you must be to me what Molière's old nurse was to him.'

"The whole or nearly all the 'Address' was read to me by him as he wrote it and a greater part if not all was written by him in my presence. The original was forwarded to Gen. Washington who approved of it with the exception of one paragraph. . . ."

The year 1796 was crucial for Hamilton. It was his first full year as a lawyer since his resignation from Washington's Cabinet. His determination to make better provision for his family is too well established by now to need elaboration. A country home that would take Elizabeth and the children out of the "pestilential area" for months at a time was a major plank in the Hamilton family-betterment program. This meant unremitting work as a lawyer.

Hamilton was true, however, to the pledge he had given President Washington when he resigned. If in any special situation he could ever be of service to Washington personally or to the country, he would make himself available.

That Hamilton did a great deal of work on the Farewell Address is clearly established by Washington's own letters to him on the subject, especially those he addressed to the former cabinet officer on August 10 and 26. In the second of these letters he states of the latest version, "I . . . prefer it greatly to the *other* drafts." Hamilton was a painstaking writer and, considering the importance of the task, one can assume that he devoted considerable time to it. Other examples could be cited of time-consuming assignments that Hamilton undertook between 1796 and 1798 when he officially resumed serving the country at the request of President Adams and Secretary McHenry. These sacrifices of time made in the public interest undoubtedly retarded his rural-retreat project.

In some of the letters dealing with The Grange acres, Hamilton refers to himself as a farmer; in others he calls himself a gardener. Among the Hamilton papers are a few memoranda, probably prepared for the guidance of his wife since he was often absent.

In the most interesting of these, there was an introductory paragraph dealing with the arrangement of flower beds and the laying out of a vegetable garden, after which he wrote:

"The Gardener, after marking these out and making a beginning by way of example, will apply himself to the planting of Raspberries in the orchard. He will go to Mr. Delafield for a supply of the English sort and if not sufficient will add from our own and some to be got from our neighbours.

"If it can be done in time I should be glad if space could be prepared in the *center* of the flower garden for planting a few tulips, hyacinths, and (missing). The space should be a circle of which the diameter is Eighteen feet: and there should be nine of each sort of flowers; but the gardener will do well to consult as to the season.

"They may be arranged thus: Wild roses around the outside of the flower garden with laurel at foot.

"If practicable I should be glad some laurel should be planted along the edge of the shrubbery and round the clump of trees near the house; also sweet briars and (illegible).

"A few dogwood trees not large, scattered along the margin of the grove would be very pleasant, but the fruit trees there must be first removed and advanced in front.

"These labours, however must not interfere with the hot bed."

Another memorandum—also in the handwriting of the master of The Grange—seems to have been a combination of things he was considering doing and things he had decided to do:

"1. Transplant fruit trees from the other side of the stable.

"2. Fences repaired. (Illegible) repaired behind stable. The cross fence at the foot of the hill? Potatoes Bradhursts? Ground may be removed and used for this purpose. Cows no longer to be permitted to range.

"3. The sod and earth which were removed in making the walks *where it is good* may be thrown upon the grounds in front of the House, and a few waggon loads of the Compost.

"4. A *Ditch* to be dug along the fruit garden and grove about four feet wide, and the earth taken upon the *sand hill* in the rear."

Although Hamilton relied mainly on Judge Peters and Dr. Hosack for agricultural and gardening guidance, he is said also to have depended in certain areas on a book published in London in 1728 which was considered authoritative by farmers and horticulturists in England, the United States, and elsewhere. The book, with its title and sub-title, was known as *New Principles of Gardening, or The Layout and Planting of Pastures, Groves, Wildernesses, Labyrinths, Avenues, Parks, etc., after a More Grand and Rural Manner Than Has Been Done Before, Illuminated with a Variety of Grand Designs.* The author himself, it was said, could not remember the full title and in time the book became known as *New Principles of Gardening.*

Among those whom the Hamiltons entertained at The Grange, in addition to such intimates as John Jay, Gouverneur Morris, Rufus King, and Judge Peters, were Nicholas Fish, Egbert Benson, John Laurance, Robert Troup, William Duer, Richard Varick, Oliver Wolcott, William Seton, Charles Wilkes, Matthew Clarkson, Richard Harrison, Elias Boudenot, Thomas Cooper, Caleb Gibbs, William Bayard, Timothy Pickering, and James Kent.

"Some of these men," we learn from *The Intimate Life,* "were associated with Hamilton in the army, and during the years he was in Congress and in the Treasury, and others were constantly engaged at the same time in the courts. So closely were his professional and public life connected, that we find

Inlaid mahogany serving table, one of a pair, made in New York City for the Hamilton Grange. *Allan McLane Hamilton Collection. U. S. National Museum*

his correspondence filled with all manner of subjects, and it is common for letters to open with an appeal to him for legal aid, and to end with some reference to politics."

As Wall Street and journeyman lawyer, host at The Grange, agricultural dilettante, dabbler in politics, and sometime contributor of articles and letters to *The Evening Post, The New York Gazette and General Advertiser, The Daily Advertiser,* and other publications, Hamilton led a busy life. Under the circumstances it is surprising that he found *any* time for relaxation.

A few years after the turn of the century, the inevitable Allan McLane Hamilton wrote:

"In Hamilton's periods of relaxation he was to be seen wandering through the woods of Harlem with a single-barreled fowling-piece, on the lookout for woodcock or other game, or he found his way to the wooded shores of his estate in search of an occasional striped bass in the clear water of the North River. Before his death he gave this gun to Trumbull [John Trumbull the artist who did the famous portrait of Hamilton at forty-five], and it ultimately

Hepplewhite shield-back chair, mahogany with satinwood inlay, originally in the formal dining room of The Grange. *Gift to The Grange of the American Scenic and Historic Preservation Society*

came into my possession. On the stock are roughly carved the letters 'A. Hamilton, N.Y.', and this was evidently his own work. When occasions were favorable, the worries of professional work, and . . . the importunities of builders, were escaped by a visit to the theatre, Hamilton and his wife going from The Grange to the city, where they were the guests of . . . friends, and they still kept a house on Partition Street. . . . According to the contemporary press, . . . among the plays produced were 'The Tragedy of Alexander the Great with a Great Heroic Spectacle of the Siege of Oxydrace,' 'The Duenna,' 'The Lyar,' 'Count Benyowski, or The Conspiracy of Kamskatka,' . . . and 'Paul & Virginia, the Plot from M. de St. Pierre's very popular novel of the same with new scenery and machinery never before exhibited,—Dance by the Negroes, the Whole to Conclude with the representation of a Tornado in which Virginia is shipwrecked, who is seen struggling in the Water while the Ship is Burnt by Lightning.' "

The Hamiltons also drove down from The Grange to attend an occasional concert of the Philharmonic Society, held at Snow's Hotel at 69 Broadway.

General Schuyler's visits to The Grange became less and less frequent because of ill health. He and Mrs. Schuyler had a standing invitation to visit the Harlem retreat and whenever they felt equal to the trip they joyfully made it; the ties of affection that bound the two families had strengthened ("if such were possible," as one relative observed) with the passing of the years.

On December 20, 1802, he sent his daughter a letter from Albany that began with a reference to the illness of one of his little grandsons:

"I hope he is now perfectly recovered, and that I shall embrace him here, as Mr. Rensselaer says you intend to accompany the General in the next month when he must be here. This will afford us additional pleasure, . . . and if the wound in my thigh and the Gout which has seized on one of my feet will permit, we will accompany you to The Grange."

A significant aspect of this letter is the revelation that the Hamiltons kept The Grange running so many months beyond the summer season; this establishes that some of the old newspaper stories which refer to it as a "summer retreat" are in error. In General Schuyler's letter late in December, we find that he refers to a visit to The Grange he hopes to make "in the next

One of a pair of English mahogany armchairs in the Chinese manner, given to Alexander Hamilton by his father-in-law, Gen. Philip Schuyler, for use at The Grange. *Allan McLane Hamilton Collection. U. S. National Museum*

month." As pointed out earlier, the Harlem house was hard to heat but the indications are that it was closed only during the coldest and bleakest weeks of winter.

One of the most spectacular days in the history of The Grange was the subject of an article in the *New York World* in 1891:

"At this house, in 1802, Hamilton gave a dinner that was largely attended by eminent statesmen. After the banquet they adjourned to the gardens sur-

The Grange about 1864. The gum trees are at the far right

rounding the house. In the presence of his guests and to symbolize the thirteen original States of the Union, Hamilton planted thirteen sapling gum trees in a group, a few rods from the manor. The event was solemnized by prayer, speech-making and all the festivities peculiar to the olden times."

Among the records at Federal Hall National Memorial in New York City there is a bill amounting to $150 for the purchase of wine by Hamilton. Fetes such as the ceremony of the thirteen trees undoubtedly involved the drinking of many toasts.

Why did Hamilton choose the gum tree? Why not some other variety? The only explanation that I have been able to find is in an unidentified clipping (the name of the publication is not given nor is the date) in the files of the New York Public Library. It reads: "The beautiful star-like leaf of the gum tree rendered it peculiarly appropriate for the purpose. . . .

"We can imagine that the patriot guarded them," the article continues, "with the tenderest care, and watched them as they slowly developed a growth which has finally become as strong and sturdy as that of the sovereignties of which they were made the emblems."

Those trees disappeared when time and souvenir-hunters joined forces. It would be exciting to see them reappear when The Grange is relocated and restored. The National Park Service will decide whether such a planting is feasible. Probably their decision will depend largely on the question of their being able to acquire enough land for the new site to accommodate the symbolic thirteen trees.

The record indicates that even a year after the Hamiltons moved into The Grange the house and grounds were still in the forefront of Hamilton's restless mind; and instructions continued to pour from his pen.

For example, on October 14, 1803, he wrote Elizabeth from Claverack, New York:

"My Dear Eliza: I arrived here this day, in about as good health as I left home though somewhat fatigued.

"There are some things necessary to be done which I omitted mentioning to you. I wish the Carpenter to make and insert two Chimnies for Ventilating the Ice-House, each about two feet square & four feet long half above and half below the ground to have a cap on the top sloping downwards so that the rain may not easily enter—the aperture for letting in and out the air to be about a foot and a half square in the side immediately below the cap (see figure on the other side).

"Let a separate compost bed be formed near the present one, to consist of 3 barrels full of *clay* which I bought, 6 barrels of *black moulds,* 2 waggon loads of the best clay on the Hill opposite the *Quakers plain* this side of Mr. Verplanks (the Gardener must go for it himself) and one waggon load of pure cowdung—Let these be well and repeatedly mixed and pounded together to be made up of hereafter for the Vines.

"I hope the apple trees will have been planted so as to profit by this moderate and wet weather. If not done, let *Tough* be reminded that a temporary fence is to be put up along the declivity of the Hill from the King's bridge road to the opposite wood so as to prevent the cattle injuring the young trees—the fence near the entrance to the Helicon Spring ought for the same reason to be attended to—The materials of the fence taken down in making the Kitchen Garden & some rubbish, which may be picked up will answer—

"Remember that the piazzas are also to be caulked & that additional accommodations for the pidgeons are to be made—

"You see I do not forget the Grange—No that I do not; nor any one that inhabits it. Accept yourself my tenderest affection—Give my love to your children & remember me to Cornelia.

Adieu my darling
A. H."

What Hamilton had in mind when he said, "see figure [the underscoring is his] on the other side," cannot be described. His drawing, diagram, informal blueprint, or whatever it happened to be, was lost forever when some vandal, visiting the Ford Collection in the Lenox Library (now the New York Public Library) decided to cut out the plan and appropriate it. Some of the letter itself was lost in the process.

Mrs. Hamilton was a conscientious correspondent who when her husband was traveling kept him supplied with news about herself, the children, and The Grange. He never seemed to run out of ideas for the improvement of the latter. She, knowing how absorbed he was in the Harlem project, made a point of acknowledging his instructions promptly and keeping him informed on their fulfillment.

Hamilton was afflicted with the familiar tensions of the man who chronically overworks, and when there was no letter from Elizabeth when he expected one, he was upset, as in this undated letter (which is identifiable as of The Grange period because of the address):

"Mrs. Elizabeth Hamilton
at Haerlem
New York.

"I was extremely disappointed, my dear Eliza, that the Monday's post did not bring me a letter from you. You used to keep your promises better. And you know that I should be anxious of your health. If the succeeding post does not rectify the omission of the former, I shall be dissatisfied and pained.

"Adieu my beloved, and be assured that I shall not lose a moment to return to you.

Yours tenderly,
A. H."

The foregoing was followed by this letter, dated only "Sunday Morning," also addressed to "Mrs. Elizabeth Hamilton, at Haerlem, New York":

"I was much relieved, my dear Eliza, by the receipt yesterday morning of your letter of Monday last. How it came to be so long delayed I am unable to conjecture. But the delay gave much uneasiness in consequence of the imperfect state of health in which I left you. I thank God you were better—for indeed, my Eliza, you are very essential to me. Your virtues more and more endear you to me and experience more and more convinces me that true happiness is only to be found in the bosom of one's own family.

"I am in hopes that I may be able to leave this place sooner than I had counted upon, say on Friday or Saturday. But I may be disappointed and may be detained till Sunday morning. This at all events I trust will bring me home on Tuesday following. The stage is three days in performing the journey. . . .

"Adieu my beloved.

A. H."

Hamilton learned what many are still discovering today, that it always costs more to build a home than originally planned; and that, as new enthusiasms develop and one finds more and more things for the builder to do, the cost keeps mounting. This probably explains why Hamilton's pattern of overwork continued and became even more pronounced. It would be interesting to reconstruct a typical Hamilton work week with the purpose of determining how many hours he put in. There is no indication that his wife had many opportunities to invoke the earlier-mentioned advice of her father, "You must, my dear child, order his horse every fair day, that he may ride out," followed by the General's little homily on the need for "bodily exercise" as an antidote for "too great an application to business."

In that unidentified article in the New York Public Library on The Grange and Hamilton's struggle to build it, we read:

"He was compelled to work hard to support the position which he was obliged to maintain, and midnight often found him working in his office. Said Talleyrand to a friend, after meeting Hamilton at this stage of his career: 'I have beheld one of the wonders of the world. I have seen a man who has made the fortune of a nation labouring all night to support his family.' "

9

The story of The Grange is in some respects a peculiar one—a jigsaw puzzle, and not always a dovetailing one. Not *intrinsically* peculiar, it has strange aspects merely because there are so many missing pieces. For instance, this letter from General Schuyler in Albany to his daughter "at Haerlem," dated April 23, 1803, yields no detectable amplification:

"Dear Child: This morning Genr. Ten Broeck informed me that your horses which went from hence were drowned, and that you had lost paint, oil, etc. to a considerable amount—Supposing this account to have been truly stated to the General, I send you by Toney my waggon horses of which I make you present.

"I intended to have your house painted. If you cannot recover the paint, purchase no more as I will have the house painted.

"When an opportunity offers send my saddle and bridle which Toney will leave . . . .

"I am Dr child

Your affectionate parent
Ph. Schuyler."

One can only speculate about the foregoing. From the spring of 1803 the Hamiltons had done considerable gala entertaining at The Grange, so undoubtedly the house had been painted when they first occupied it in August, 1802. Perhaps it had been given an initial coat, which could have needed retouching after being subjected to the blasts and low temperatures of that first winter.

Hamilton enjoyed the role of host, which was fortunate, since he "owed" dinners to so many friends. Having become part of the social life of New

Inlaid mahogany table in the Louis XVI style, made in 1802 or 1803 for The Grange. *Allan McLane Hamilton Collection. U. S. National Museum*

York, he and Elizabeth received frequent dinner invitations. Much of this popularity stemmed from Hamilton's political prominence; and though many an invitation could not be accepted because the master of The Grange was away from New York, the Hamiltons managed to be reasonably active socially.

By 1803 there was something to talk about besides politics—for instance, the emergence of Harlem as a community, which, despite its being a considerable distance from New York's business district, was beginning to impress more and more people as a locale that probably had a future. It was still thinly populated, although more and more people were looking at building sites and some of them found what they wanted. Hamilton could even point to Harlem's first fire engine and plans being urged by residents for additional roads and the improvement of existing ones.

It may be assumed that, in addition to politics and the steady growth of Harlem, Hamilton's guests had something to say about some of the clients he advised on legal and business matters. Especially interesting were the cases that found their way into the newspaper columns. A good conversation-maker was *The New York Evening Post,* which Hamilton founded with the help of fellow Federalists who felt that the decline of their party was at least partly due to the lack of a strong Federalist newspaper in New York. Hamilton himself was able to contribute only about $1,000 to the venture but he named the editor and influenced policy. By the time socializing and entertaining were in full swing at The Grange the new paper was over a year old, and presumably what it published—much of it controversial—was discussed at the dinner table since most of Hamilton's guests were Federalists.

About two and a half years after it was founded, the *Post* and Hamilton parted company politically. The date was March 23, 1804. This was a crushing blow to Hamilton. He and his Federalist intimates must have given so sensational a development a good conversational workout when they gathered at The Grange.

During this period Hamilton was selected as business consultant to a man whose industry and imagination were beginning to attract attention, a Mr. E. I. duPont. It was Hamilton's advice that led to the selection of a site near Wilmington, Delaware, for the duPont manufacturing plant; and presumably the exploits of this newsworthy client made good table talk, too, for it was generally conceded that duPont was a "doer," as one of his contemporaries put it.

According to one authority, "a feature of both formal and family gatherings at The Grange was the piano playing and singing of daughter Angelica, accompanied by her father. Whether the father sang as well as played accompaniment is not clear."

In his diary Gouverneur Morris refers to a children's party at The Grange in May of 1804:

". . . Go between two and three to Genl Hamilton's to a Fete given to his Daughter's Acquaintances and return without being wet though it constantly threatens. . . ."

The Hamiltons had two daughters: Eliza, who was not quite five at the time, and Angelica, who was between nineteen and twenty; undoubtedly the "daughter" to whom Morris alluded was Angelica.

One of Hamilton's friends was James Kent, a distinguished jurist who served as professor of law at Columbia College before receiving an appointment as master in chancery. He and Hamilton, both perceptive students of the law as applied to the needs of a new, developing country, took every opportunity they could find to compare notes and exchange views on their favorite subject.

In a letter to his wife Chancellor Kent describes a visit to The Grange in April, 1804:

"I went out with General Hamilton on Saturday, the 21st, and stayed till Sunday evening. There was a furious and dreadful storm on Saturday night. It blew almost a hurricane. His house stands high, and was much exposed, and I am certain that in the second story, where I slept, it rocked like a cradle.

"He never appeared before so friendly and amiable. I was alone, and he treated me with a minute attention that I did not suppose he knew how to bestow. His manners were also very delicate and chaste. His daughter is nineteen years old, has a very uncommon simplicity and modesty of deportment, and he appeared in his domestic state the plain, modest, and affectionate father and husband."

Noteworthy among the more dazzling evenings at The Grange was a formal dinner for the youngest brother of Napoleon, Jerome Bonaparte, who had served in his country's navy and was sent to the West Indies. He secured his brother's permission to visit the United States, where in 1803 he met and married Elizabeth Patterson of Baltimore. In the spring of the following year the Hamiltons entertained Jerome Bonaparte and his lady at The Grange.

From his office or the Hamilton town house, on May 7 Hamilton wrote his wife at The Grange:

"On Sunday Bonaparte & Wife with the Judges will dine with you. We shall be 16 in number if Gouverneur Morris will come. Send him the inclosed note on horseback, this Evening, that James may bring me an answer in the morning. He is promised the little horse to return.

"If not prevented by the cleaning of your house I hope the pleasure of seeing you tomorrow.

"Let the waggon as well as the coaches come in on Saturday. I mention this now, lest you should not come to town yourself. I have particular reasons for this request."

It is interesting to note that apparently Hamilton did the inviting himself, no doubt with the blessing of Mrs. Hamilton, who cheerfully followed her husband's lead.

The phrase "this Evening" in the first paragraph indicates that Hamilton did not mail this letter, but that he undoubtedly dispatched it to The Grange by special courier.

Toasts were drunk that Sunday night to young Bonaparte and his American wife; and to some who attended these festivities at the Hamilton country home they must have seemed a happy augury of improved Franco-American relations. However, these people were reckoning without France's ruler, Napoleon, to whom the young man was answerable. On Jerome's return to France, the ruler of the French Empire said that he did not recognize his brother's American marriage and he made a new match for Jerome with Catherine of Württemberg before naming him King of Westphalia. Over thirty years later Jerome Bonaparte, inspired by recollections of the gala in his honor at The Grange, entertained Hamilton's son James in Florence, Italy, "midst much pomp and formality."

During the summer months Hamilton avoided the heat of his downtown office as much as possible; when feasible he worked in his study at The Grange which was cooled by the breezes of the Hudson. Here he also engaged in one of his favorite pastimes, straightening out the record. This would usually take the form of a letter to the editor of a newspaper. Customarily the identification at the beginning of the missive would be "At Haerlem" and he would sign himself "Pericles," "An American," or whatever seemed suitable at the moment.

Attacking a rumor involving himself and others that had been published, he wrote a letter to the editor of the *New York Post.* Here is an excerpt:

". . . The story imports in substance that General Lafayette, with the approbation or connivance of General Washington ordered me, as the officer who was to command the attack on a British redoubt, in the course of the Siege of York Town, to put to death all those of the enemy who should happen to be taken in the redoubt, and that through motives of humanity, I forbore to execute the order.

"Positively and unequivocally I declare that no such order . . . was ever by me received."

Two months after the festive dinner party in honor of the Jerome Bonapartes, Hamilton left The Grange—the date was July 11, 1804—to meet Aaron Burr at the Weehawken, New Jersey, dueling ground where his son Philip had been killed two years before.

He wrote his wife two farewell letters, one on July 4, the other on July 10, but how these letters reached her, or by whom they were delivered, is not known. Both were addressed to The Grange, where the family was in residence for the summer.

These dueling pistols, stolen from The Grange when it was a museum, are not the ones actually used by Hamilton and Burr in their tragic encounter. They are thought to have been an extra pair kept in readiness, in accordance with dueling practice

The first read:

"This letter, my very dear Eliza, will not be delivered to you unless I shall first have terminated my earthly career, to begin, as I humbly hope, from redeeming grace and divine mercy, a happy immortality.

"If it had been possible for me to have avoided the interview, my love for you and my precious children would have been alone a decisive motive. But it was not possible, without sacrifices which would have rendered me unworthy of your esteem. I need not tell you of the pangs I feel from the idea of quitting you, and exposing you to the anguish which I know you would feel. Nor could I dwell on the topic lest it should unman me.

"The consolation of Religion, my beloved, can alone support you; and these you have a right to enjoy. Fly to the bosom of your God and be comforted.

"With my last idea I shall cherish the sweet hope of meeting you in a better world.

"Adieu best of wives—best of women.

"Embrace all my darling children for me.

Ever yours,
A. H."

The second letter was:

"My Beloved Eliza: Mrs. Mitchell is the person in the world to whom as a friend I am under the greatest obligations. (*Note: Mrs. Mitchell was an aged aunt who lived in Burlington, New Jersey.*)

"I have not hitherto done my duty to her. But resolved to repair my omission to her as much as possible . . . and intend, if it shall be in my power, to render the evening of her days comfortable.

"But if it shall please God to put this out of my power, I entreat you to do it, and to treat her with the tenderness of a sister. . . .

"The scruples of a Christian have determined me to expose my own life to any extent rather than subject myself to the guilt of taking the life of another. This much increases my hazards, and redoubles my pangs for you.

"But you had rather I should die innocent than live guilty. Heaven can preserve me, and I humbly hope will; but in the contrary event I charge you to remember that you are a Christian. God's will be done!

"The will of a merciful God must be good. Once more,

"Adieu my darling, darling wife.

A. H."

Many years later, Hamilton's son John, who was thirteen years of age in July, 1804, wrote:

"The day before the duel I was sitting in a room (at The Grange) when at a slight noise I turned and saw my father in the doorway standing silently looking at me with a most sweet and beautiful expression of countenance, full of tenderness and without any of the business preoccupations he sometimes had.

" 'John,' said he, 'won't you come and sleep with me tonight,' and his voice was frank as if it had been my brother's instead of my father's. That night I went to his bed and in the morning very early he awakened me and taking my hands in his palms, all four hands extended, he told me to repeat the Lord's Prayer.

"Seventy years have since passed over my head, and I have forgotten many things, but not that tender expression when he stood looking at me at the door, nor the prayer we made together the morning just before the duel."

According to the chronicler of your choice, it was two, three, or four o'clock of the morning of July 11 that Hamilton left The Grange to confront Burr in Weehawken.

When Burr's bullet struck him in the side, Hamilton, mortally wounded, was taken to the home of his friend William Bayard (one of the first to be invited to The Grange) at 80 Jane Street in New York. Dr. Hosack, the family doctor, had accompanied Hamilton on the boat that took him to Weehawken. Hosack, who, it will be recalled, was one of Hamilton's advisers in matters horticultural and agricultural, knew what The Grange meant to his friend and had the wound been less serious he probably would have taken him to the Harlem retreat; but, according to newspaper accounts, it was not believed Hamilton could survive so taxing a trip. He died the following afternoon in "a large, square room on the second floor of Mr. Bayard's house."

10

Mrs. Hamilton occupied The Grange for many years after her husband's death. There are letters written by her as late as 1819, beginning with the familiar "at Harlem" or "at The Grange" designations.

Her son James reports in his *Reminiscences* that she spent her remaining years in Washington, D. C., where she died at ninety-seven in 1854, fifty years after her husband's death. Possessions—three in particular—that had occupied places of honor at The Grange were now to be found in her new home. Here is a passage from a neighbor's written description:

"The side wall near the entrance door was almost covered with a large half-length portrait of Washington, who sat to Stuart for it, and gave it to Hamilton. Under a large handsome centre table in the front parlor was a great silver wine-cooler, also a gift from Washington. I remember nothing more distinctly than a sofa and chairs with spindle legs, upholstered in black broadcloth, embroidered in flowery wreaths by Mrs. Hamilton herself, and a marble bust of Hamilton standing on its pedestal. . . . That bust I can never forget, for the old lady always paused before it in her tour of the rooms, and, leaning on her cane, gazed and gazed, as if she could never be satisfied."

It had previously been reported by visitors to The Grange that for years after Hamilton's death, and until Mrs. Hamilton found the Harlem retreat too expensive to maintain and sold it, she frequently went through the same silent ritual when she found herself passing that bust—the work of the Italian sculptor Giuseppi Ceracchi. It is in the United States National Museum today, the gift of Hamilton Murray.

The Grange was sold in 1833 for $25,000. The purchaser was Moses Henriques, an agent representing a client of a banking firm. The property was immediately conveyed to a real estate speculator, one Theodore E. Davis. Davis sold the property in 1835 to Isaac G. Pearson for $52,511.

A few years later Pearson was declared bankrupt and Samuel Ward (who was related to Julia Ward Howe) emerged as the new owner. Different branches of the Ward family occupied The Grange until 1876.

The heirs of William Ward lost the property by foreclosure to the Emigrant Industrial Savings Bank; the sum due the bank, which the Wards could not

One of the treasures of The Grange: "Washington" by Gilbert Stuart, presented by Washington to Alexander Hamilton. *The New York Public Library. Gift of a Hamilton descendant*

Marble portrait bust of Alexander Hamilton done from life by Giuseppe Ceracchi. This sculpture was removed from The Grange by Mrs. Hamilton and installed in her home in Washington, D. C., where she went to live some years after her husband's death. *U. S. National Museum. Gift of Hamilton Murray*

Marble portrait bust of Alexander Hamilton done from life by Giuseppe Ceracchi. This sculpture was removed from The Grange by Mrs. Hamilton and installed in her home in Washington, D. C., where she went to live some years after her husband's death. *U. S. National Museum. Gift of Hamilton Murray*

raise, was $53,402. In 1879 the bank sold The Grange to one Anthony Mowbray, an agent, for $312,500. Mowbray conveyed it to the men he represented, William H. De Forest and his son William H., Jr. Their primary interest was the land Hamilton had bought for his country home a little over three-quarters of a century earlier from the Schieffelins and the Bradhursts. The De Forests, downtown merchants, converted Hamilton's land into 300 building lots, which were sold for $5,000 each, or a total of $1,500,000.

Dozens of pages could be devoted to the vicissitudes of The Grange under different ownerships but much of this information is not particularly pertinent or interesting. On the other hand, there are colorful developments in the history of the Hamilton house which, because of the points they make, demand telling. One such is to be found in the December, 1924 issue of *The St. Luke's Family Magazine,* published under the auspices of Trinity Church which administered St. Luke's. These passages give the gist of the full account:

"In the autumn of 1889 it happened that the rector of Saint Luke's Church in Hudson Street (the Rev. Isaac H. Tuttle) was reconnoitering the vicinity for an empty building suitable in which to gather the nucleus of a congregation for the new Saint Luke's about to be erected on Convent Avenue and 141st Street. Observing on Convent Avenue, approximately three hundred feet north of the new church site, a large, old-fashioned frame dwelling that had the appearance of former glory and elegance, he made inquiry as to its present ownership.

"To his surprise he learned that the house had been built and occupied by Alexander Hamilton and that its present owner was a Mr. Amos Cotting.

"A mutual acquaintance arranged a luncheon for the rector to meet Mr. Cotting. When Dr. Tuttle explained his desire to rent the house, and the purpose he had in mind, Mr. Cotting without hesitancy, generously offered to make it a deed of gift to him. The house was moved to the east side of Convent Avenue and placed upon land bought by the church corporation." (In purchasing the site for the new church, a more than ample parcel of land was acquired, and it was part of this surplus ground that was used to accommodate The Grange, which has stood beside the church ever since.)

And now to resume quoting from the story in the church publication:

"Somehow the feeling prevailed that it (The Grange) was not worth preserving, which created a positive reluctance (on the part of the vestry and churchwardens) to spend any money on it. But Doctor Tuttle thought otherwise. In the first place the house had been the home of the nation's first Secretary of the Treasury. Its timbers were of white oak and hand-hewn . . . and were still substantial, far surpassing the foundations of some modern dwellings. . . .

"Dr. Tuttle was firmly convinced the house repaired would continue useful to the church for many years. . . .

"The structure was much in need of repair and required an entire new roof."

According to *The History of St. Luke's Church in the City of New York,* published in 1926, the "inadequate resources of the (St. Luke's) treasury," due to the cost of the new church, made it necessary for Tuttle to find some other means of financing the urgently needed repairs. He offered to pay for them himself and the church accepted. A new tin roof alone cost Tuttle $1,500.

The record clearly indicates that Tuttle was the savior of The Grange. If not for his foresight, determination, and generosity it is doubtful whether the Hamilton house would be standing today.

In 1924 The Grange was conveyed to the American Scenic and Historic Preservation Society through a gift of $100,000 for purchase and maintenance by J. P. Morgan and George F. Baker, Jr. Half this sum was the actual purchase price, the other $50,000 was set up as a trust fund, the income of which was to be used for maintenance.

In 1933, after extensive renovation, it was opened as a Hamilton Museum. The funds for maintenance must have been inadequate; at any rate, deterioration set in and twenty years later the shabbiness of the building was so apparent that The Grange became a virtually unvisited museum. The paint was peeling inside and out, and the plaster was falling from the ceilings; so people stayed away. Some days there were no visitors, and it reached the point where, if five or six people showed up, it was considered a big day.

The Grange is now owned by the Federal government, which would seem highly appropriate to a dedicated Federalist like Hamilton. In 1962, Congress, under a bill introduced by the then Representative John V. Lindsay, declared the house a national memorial and appropriated $460,000 for its restoration and rehabilitation.

The problem has been to find a suitable site for it.

Ingloriously, the old house stands today at Convent Avenue and 141st Street. It is tightly squeezed in the shadow formed by St. Luke's Episcopal Church on the south and an apartment house on the north. Architect McComb would lie uneasy in his grave if he knew what this crowding has done to the grace and dignity of his original concept.

The *New York Times* on October 26, 1966, carried a story by John C. Devlin that opened with these paragraphs:

"A Manhattan clergyman said yesterday that he was writing to President Johnson to charge the Federal Government with 'dilatory tactics' in saving the derelict-like old manor house of Alexander Hamilton, a national memorial since 1962.

"The clergyman, the Rev. David Johnson, who is the Rector of St. Luke's Episcopal Church, said he was also appealing to Secretary of the Interior Stewart L. Udall for 'long-delayed action' in saving the crumbling structure."

This is the kind of plain talk that appealed to Alexander Hamilton. In fact, if he, Rufus King, and other Federalists had succeeded in getting into the Constitution a clause mentioned earlier in these pages, President Johnson, if he agreed with Reverend Johnson (and it is hard to imagine his taking an opposite view), could have written the rector of St. Luke's approximately as follows: "You will be glad to know that on receiving your letter, I issued an executive order calling for the immediate restoration of The Grange. If the $460,000 appropriated by Congress proves insufficient I will issue a second executive order, this one empowering Interior to spend whatever is required."

Here is an eloquent representation of "gracious living" at The Grange:

"Old accounts tell us of the gracious entertainment which the Hamilton family provided their distinguished guests. Fine silver, worthy examples of the Sheraton and Hepplewhite furniture, graceful mantel ornaments, and fine crystal chandeliers lent grace and distinction to the handsome interior. The doorway, flanked with glass panels, remains unchanged, even to the great lock, key and brass doorknob. Many visitors to The Grange have described the famous octagonal dining room, its lofty chamber lighted by great windows opening onto the veranda.

"The architecture might be classified as a simplified expression of late classic based freely on the Adams style of England, which was evolved in the latter half of the 18th century. In other words, it is an American interpretation of its prototype. . . .

"The design of The Grange is simple but dignified. It is today one of a very few Federal period houses still standing in New York City. . . .

"The refined character of the classic frieze and the cornice of the exterior, the delicate treatment of the ornamental plaster cornices on the interior, and the elegant mantel pieces clearly signify that this was the home of a cultured gentleman. His natural discernment and that of his wife were everywhere in evidence in the dignified interior of this country mansion.

"During the time the Hamiltons lived in The Grange, they seem to have

Sheraton chairs from the family dining room at The Grange, inherited by the present Alexander Hamilton

enjoyed their country retreat. The large octagon dining room witnessed pleasant gatherings of Hamilton's friends and associates in politics, business and science. General Schuyler and his sons and daughters with husbands, wives and children were frequent visitors, and there were merry gatherings in the big house and on the sunny eastern slope among the old trees."

The "old accounts" from which the foregoing was drawn in 1957 on the two-hundredth anniversary of the birth of Hamilton conjure up pulse-quickening pictures of a historic past that fade out ignominiously when one looks at The Grange today.

Daily a steady stream of students from the nearby College of the City of New York passes The Grange. These young men and women are in the main conscious of history and since Alexander Hamilton's erstwhile country home is part of the neighborhood it is not surprising that they should stop and try to find out "what is going on" when they see activity outside the building—perhaps a workman making a minor repair or visitors entering or leaving the premises.

Early last spring (1967) Eric Sloane and I were leaving after one of our periodic visits to The Grange. Raleigh Henry Daniels, the caretaker, strolled out with us. I was jotting something down in a notebook while Mr. Sloane and Mr. Daniels chatted. A student—one of a passing group—strolled over to greet me and when he learned that we were working on a book about The Grange he began asking questions, including this one: "Why after all these years hasn't the government begun the job of restoration?" The key to his dissatisfaction was the phrase "after all these years." He knew that The Grange was Federally administered—through the Interior Department's National Park Service—but he mistakenly thought that the government had acquired the Hamilton house some time in the 1890s. He was surprised to learn that the house had not been conveyed to the United States until 1962. He pondered a moment, then observed, "Even so, they've had five years in which to rehabilitate it."

I explained that I had had the same reaction on first becoming acquainted with the problem; but that as time went on I gained some insights into the complications involving relocation and restoration. For instance, one group argued effectively for a site near Grant's Tomb, overlooking Hamilton's beloved Hudson River. This would have permitted plenty of walking room around the structure and on the whole their case was plausible and reasonably compelling. Another group insisted that The Grange was a Harlem institution, not a mere footnote to the area's history, and that to move it beyond the boundaries of Harlem would be depriving that section of the city of a significant item in its cultural inventory.

Countless petitioners made their opinions known to the proper authorities in Washington. The various views on relocation—only two of many have been cited—were weighed and considered and this took a great deal of time.

The student listened patiently for a while, then, with the impetuosity of youth, made his pronouncement: Yes, the government had problems, he realized that, but five years is a long time and he thought that there was no reason for "horsing around" any longer. This view is temperate by comparison with other comments that one hears in the area; some of the observations on the steady deterioration of The Grange while the question of a new site is being decided are more vehemently expressed.

To paraphrase William Cowper, democracy works in tardy ways its wonders to perform. It is one of the inevitabilities of a system that demands of public officials that they listen to the people. Sometimes they have to do a tremendous amount of listening before they feel free to act.

Short story writers and novelists, who for over a century have used Hamilton as a central or incidental figure, have had a lot of fun scrambling the facts. Creative writers have always been conceded a certain amount of license. Perhaps it all started when Shakespeare endowed Julius Caesar's Rome with clocks. At any rate, in one of the fictitious stories we find Hamilton and Burr meeting at a dinner party in the historic Jumel Mansion, which still stands at 160th Street and Edgecomb Avenue, New York's so-called Washington Heights section.

Actually it was not until 1810—six years after Hamilton's death—that Stephen Jumel, a rich wine dealer, bought the house from Roger Morris, one of New York's most successful merchants, who had built it as a summer home. Jumel had purchased the house for his wife, the irrepressible Eliza, best known for what one historian describes as her "irrational and short-lived marriage after Jumel's death to Aaron Burr."

Fiction has stopped short of placing Burr inside The Grange.

One anecdote, hitherto unpublished and having the ring of authenticity, has turned up that provides what could be called a floricultural link between Burr and the Hamilton country seat. The story is to be found in what Barbara P. Boucot, of the Department of Manuscripts of the Huntington Library at San Marino, describes as a "three-page manuscript by an unknown person."

The anecdote has to do with a client of Aaron Burr's—an unidentified woman simply designated as Mrs. Q.—who had called at The Grange in response to a request from the widowed Mrs. Hamilton for assistance in connection with the financing of a school in which she was interested, the implication being that Mrs. Q. was in a position to help.

"On arriving at the seat (The Grange) she (Mrs. Q.) found that Mrs. Hamilton was absent from the home, but was invited to remain for tea by the rest of the family. After the evening meal, a walk was proposed round the grounds, when her attention was attracted by a beautiful bower entwined with the most luscious honeysuckle. They told her it was a favourite retreat of Mrs. Hamilton, as it had been planted by her husband, and that even a deranged daughter knew and loved it as the frequent haunt of her beloved father. Blossoms and branches were, of course, immediately plucked as souvenirs of the General, and, on arriving at home Mrs. Q. deposited the cherished spoils in vases on her mantel.

"The next day she was in the midst of her (household) labours when Burr (her attorney) was announced.

". . . Burr . . . transacted the professional business upon which he had called. . . .

" 'And, by the way, Madam,' said he as he rose to depart and walked up to the vases of honeysuckle, 'where did you get those exquisite flowers?' Mrs. Q. says she felt like sinking through the floor. . . .

" 'I hope 'tis no theft, no piracy, no robbery, Madam!', continued he with his usual air of gallantry as he took a couple of sprigs from the water; and, making his bow, left the room, *weaving through his button holes the flowers that grew from the planting of the man he had slain.*"

This little story seems in character with the rest of Hamilton's life, described by one writer as a study in irony.

Depending on how much land is available when the new site for The Grange is finally selected, the National Park Service will probably try to duplicate at least part of the original Grange garden, as planned and augmented by Hamilton himself, including a splash of honeysuckle, perhaps the red and the white varieties as a match for the stripes of the flag that will undoubtedly fly near the entrance of the restored Hamilton country house.

Acknowledgments and Bibliography

Grateful acknowledgment is made to the Department of the Interior for making available three reports on The Grange, prepared by Alfred Mongin, Newton P. Bevin, and the New York City staff of the National Park Service, under the auspices of the last-named organization.

And a word of thanks to Larry Zollar, also of the National Park Service, and his associates in the New York City office of that division of the Department of the Interior.

Acknowledgment is also made of the helpfulness of the present-day Alexander Hamilton, great-great-grandson of his historic namesake and President of the American Scenic and Historic Preservation Society; of Dr. Gerald McDonald, Chief of American History, New York Public Library (old newspaper and magazine articles were made available by some of its other subdivisions); of the Henry E. Huntington Library, San Marino, California; and of the Museum of the City of New York.

Reminiscences by James A. Hamilton.

Alexander Hamilton: Youth to Maturity by Broadus Mitchell.

Alexander Hamilton by Nathan Schachner.

Dictionary of American Biography.

The History of St. Luke's Church in the City of New York by Mrs. H. Crosswell Tuttle, privately printed in 1926 (made available through the courtesy of The Rev. David Johnson, rector of the present-day St. Luke's Episcopal Church, which borders on The Grange).

The Works of Alexander Hamilton edited by H. C. Lodge

The Iconography of Manhattan Island by Isaac N. P. Stokes

The Life and Correspondence of Rufus King by Charles R. King

The Intimate Life of Alexander Hamilton by Allan McLane Hamilton (the book that contains the most information about The Grange).

The Epic of New York City by Edward Robb Ellis.